THE
LONDON
BOOK
OF
DAYS

PETER DE LORIOL

First published 2013

The History Press
The Mill, Brimscombe Port
Stroud, Gloucestershire, GL5 2QG
www.thehistorypress.co.uk

British Library Cataloguing in Publication Data.
A catalogue record for this book is available from the British Library.

ISBN 978 0 7524 7939 2

Typesetting and origination by The History Press
Printed in India

January 1st

1660: On this day Samuel Pepys (1633-1703) started his diary.

---◆---

1788: The first edition of the *The Times*, previously the *Daily Universal Register*, was published.

---◆---

1845: Police used the Telegraph to signal that a suspect for the murder of Sarah Hart had boarded a train at Slough, bound for Paddington. Since the Telegraph could still not send the letter 'Q', the message famously contained the description of the man as being 'in the garb of a Kwaker'. John Tawell was caught and found guilty. (*The Times*)

---◆---

1913: London's motorised cabmen went on a long strike against the price they were charged for petrol. The strike ended on 18 March when they agreed to pay 8*d* a gallon. (*Daily Mail*)

---◆---

2000: The Millennium Dome opened to the public on this day. Building this involved the reclamation of the entire Greenwich peninsula. It was conceived in 1994 under John Major's government to celebrate 3 millennia, and was used as a Labour achievement. (*Daily Mail*)

January 2nd

1818: On this day three young engineers, Henry R. Palmer, James Jones and Joshua Field, organised an inaugural meeting to found an Institute for civil engineers. The far-sighted appointment of Thomas Telford as first president enabled the Institute to attract membership and obtain a Royal Charter in the same year. (ICE Archives)

1911: Following a botched attempt by supposed Latvian thieves to break into the rear of a jeweller's shop at No. 119 Houndsditch on 16 December 1910, and the ensuing gun fight (which resulted in the death of at least one police officer and the escape of some of the gunmen), an informant told the police that members of this gang, including 'Peter The Painter', the well-known anarchist, had holed up at No. 100 Sidney Street, Stepney. The resulting gun battle the next day between 200 police officers and the gunmen, with Mr Winston Churchill in attendance, was filmed. (*Guardian*)

1982: Erika Roe streaked across Twickenham stadium during an England *v.* Australia rugby union match. Australia lost whilst Erika's memorable streak made her a suitable icon for sports interruptions. (*Independent*)

January 3rd

1804: Twenty-nine-year-old Francis Smith, one of a group of citizens patrolling the Hammersmith area in the wake of the sighting of a ghostly figure, shot and killed a plasterer, Thomas Millwood, who was wearing the pale clothes of his trade, in the evening. Smith was tried for wilful murder on the grounds of 'Intent to Kill'. Found guilty, the initial sentence of hanging and dissection was commuted to a year's hard labour.

———•◆•———

1946: William Joyce, 'Lord Haw-Haw', an Irish-American fascist who held a British passport, and who had broadcast German propaganda from Germany to Britain during the Second World War, was hanged by Albert Pierrepoint at Wandsworth Prison on this day. He was the penultimate person to be hanged for a crime other than murder. (*The Times*)

January 4th

1650: At 7 p.m., twenty-seven barrels of gunpowder stored by the wall of All Hallows Barking by the Tower, exploded, killing at least sixty-seven people and destroying fifty houses (Stow)

1698: On this day Whitehall was burnt down. (Luttrell)

1792: The first four students attended the Veterinary College in the parish of St Pancras, to begin a three-year course covering all aspects of the veterinary art. Charles Vial de St Bel, a Frenchman, was its founder and first professor.

1946: Theodore Schurch, a British soldier of Anglo-Swiss parentage, turned by the Axis forces on his capture, was hanged by Albert Pierrepoint at Pentonville Prison. He was the last person to be hanged for a crime other than murder. (*The Times*)

1969: Police raided an empty flat in Sloane Court West, Chelsea, and recovered paintings by Picasso, Dufy, Chagall and Rouault amongst others, stolen from a house in Eaton Square two weeks previously – all on a nod from an informer who overheard thieves boasting of a £150,000 art theft! (*Daily Mail*)

JANUARY 5TH

1766: The first Christie's sale occurred on this day at James Christie's rented rooms in Pall Mall. The business boomed, especially during the Revolution when French aristocrats parted with their treasures to finance their life in London! (*Chamber's Book of Days*)

———•◆•———

1851: By this date there were 159 London newspapers in which appeared 891, 650 advertisements weekly.

———•◆•———

2003: Police raided a flat above a pharmacy at No. 325 High Road, Wood Green, and arrested six men on suspicion of manufacturing ricin intended for use in a terrorist poison attack on the underground. No ricin was found, nor were many government departments made aware of the fact. The Press was gagged – it was only two years later that these facts emerged. (*Argus*)

January 6th

1651: Fifth Monarchists, headed by Thomas Venner, followers of a belief that four ancient monarchies would precede Christ's return, attempted to capture London in the name of 'King Jesus'. Most of the fifty were killed or put to death.

1772: The elderly Mrs Golding's house at Stockwell erupted in a series of kitchen utensils, food and furniture flying across rooms as if by magic. 'In her fright Mrs Golding ran into a neighbour's house and fainted and was soon afterwards bled.' Everything stopped when the servant, Ann Robinson, wasn't at home. She was sacked and everything went back to normal. (*Topographical History of Surrey,* E. Brayley)

1792: The last known notice of the Anacreontic Society, a group devoted to good music, was published in *The Times* on this day. 'To Anacreon in Heaven', the club anthem, was sung at all venues. Its music, composed by John Stafford Smith, was adopted by American rebels for the 'Star-Spangled Banner'. The latter was made the US national anthem by congressional resolution on 3 March 1931. (*The Times*)

1931: The fourth Sadler's Wells theatre opened on this day with Lilian Bayliss in a production of *Twelfth Night.* (*The Times*)

1965: Ronald and Reginald Kray, the East End gang-leaders, were remanded in custody on this day and charged with demanding money with menace. (*Daily Mail*)

JANUARY 7TH

1618: Sir Francis Bacon, one of the most naturally gifted men, was made Lord Chancellor of England today by his patron James I.

———◆———

1714: Henry Mill, a waterworks engineer working for the New River Co. which channelled water to London, submitted a patent on this day, No. 395, for a 'machine for transcribing letters'. The machine he invented appears to be the precursor to the modern typewriter built many years later! (Patent Office)

———◆———

1928: Heavy snow, followed by a sudden thaw, and heavy rain combined with a high spring tide and a storm surge raised the water levels on the Thames, producing the highest water levels ever recorded in the Thames in London. It created a massive flood which overflowed the embankment from the City to Putney and Hammersmith. Fourteen people drowned and 4,000 people were made homeless. Disaffected areas were destroyed and rebuilt, and the disaster contributed to the eventual building of the Thames Barrier. (*Daily Mail*)

January 8th

1991: A commuter train from Sevenoaks crashed at Cannon Street Station. Two carriages concertinaed, killing one person and injuring hundreds. (*Evening Standard*)

———•◆•———

1806: Lord Nelson's body was carried by state barge on the Thames from Greenwich to Whitehall. Church bells rang, canons fired and spectators lined the shores and bridges. The body was then carried to the Admiralty and was taken to St Paul's the next day for burial. (*The Times*)

———•◆•———

1960: Stanley Wilson, a thirty-three-year-old divorcé and teacher in Fulham, pleaded guilty to a charge of knowingly permitting his house to be used for prostitution. He had taken in two homeless girls for whom he had found jobs, but one found that prostitution from home was more remunerative. He was fined £30. (*The Times*)

———•◆•———

1734: George Friedrich Handel's *Ariodante* premiered at the Royal Opera House to rapturous applause on this day. Despite its initial success, it fell into oblivion for the next 200 years until it was revived in New York. (*London Daily Post*)

JANUARY 9TH

1957: On this day Sir Anthony Eden, the conservative politician, resigned as Prime Minister because of ill health. He had been Prime Minister for 1 year and 279 days. Harold MacMillan succeeded him. (*Observer*)

1930: On this day there were further increases of smallpox in London. The isolation hospitals of the Metropolitan Asylum board reported 442 patients under treatment. The number of admissions to hospital was thirty-seven, of 'which five were from West Ham'; of those already in hospital eighty-four were also from West Ham. (*The Times*)

1930: On the same day the Duveen room, a gift from Sir Joseph Duveen, was opened at the National Gallery by Prince George. (*The Times*)

1838: On this day a resident of Peckham addressed a letter to the Lord Mayor saying that a rich young wag was scaring people in the guise of a ghost, a bear and a devil for a bet, and that seven ladies had been scared out of their wits. The resident wrote that these ladies 'have the whole history at their finger ends, but, through interested motives, are induced to remain silent'. (*The Times*)

January 10th

1985: A gas blast in the early morning killed eight people in Newnham House, a three-storey block of flats on the Manor Fields Estate in Putney Hill. (*Daily Mail*)

———◆———

1863: The Metropolitan Railway, an underground railway between Paddington Station and Farrington Street, was formally opened on this day. This was the world's first commercial underground, and 26,000 passengers went on it within a few months. (*The Times*)

———◆———

1930: George Buchanan wrote to *The Times* regarding the traffic and pedestrians on this day; he suggested that cars issuing onto main roads such as Piccadilly, from side streets, should obligatorily honk their horns – pedestrians should only cross streets at specified crossings. He noted that in Paris it is a punishable offence to cross outside a pedestrian marking. He also advocated a 25-30mph speed limit!

JANUARY 11TH

1569: Drawing of the winning tickets of the first lottery in England continued until 6 May. It was a perfect way for the state to raise cash. This took place at the western door of St Paul's Cathedral. It contained 40,000 lots at 10s each lot; the profits were for repairing harbours and the prizes were pieces of plate. (Stow)

1804: On this day Francis Small was indicted for the murder of Thomas Millwood, the Hammersmith Ghost. (*See* January 3rd.) (LB Fulham and Hammersmith Archives)

1864: Charing Cross Station was opened on this day. The original station building was built on the site of the Hungerford Market by South Eastern Railway. The station had a single-span, wrought-iron roof arching over the six platforms on its site. It was built on a brick-arched viaduct. The Charing Cross Hotel opened on 15 May 1865 (one year later) and gave the station an ornate frontage in the French Renaissance style. (*The Times*)

1941: The Luftwaffe attacked London, dropping bombs on Covent Garden Market and Bow Street police station.

JANUARY 12TH

1789: Melting ice dragged at a ship anchored to a Thames riverside public house, pulling down the building and causing five people to be crushed to death. (*The Times*)

———•———

1827: This Friday the *Morning Chronicle* related the tale of the book dealer of New Road whose twelve-year-old son had quarrelled with two women in the court in which he lived and threw dirt in their faces. He was taken to Marlborough Street Office to be tried at the Sessions for assault. His father came to pay the bail of £5, but it was too late as the son had been taken to prison. The son was released upon payment, but the Clerk of the Peace returned the money to the father because he was so ashamed of the matter.

———•———

1989: Great Ormond Street Children's Hospital announced that it had achieved its target of £42 million for redevelopment a year ahead of schedule – the biggest appeal of its kind launched in Britain. (*The Times*)

January 13th

1583: Eight people were killed on this day at Paris Gardens, to the west of Southwark, when the scaffolds crowded with people watching bear-baiting collapsed. It was considered God's wrath as it happened on the Sabbath. (Southwark History Archives)

———•◆•———

1612: A Session House, the first purpose-built Court House in Middlesex, was opened on this day in St John Street, Clerkenwell, through the munificence of Sir Baptist Hicks. (City of London Records Office)

———•◆•———

1785: Mr John Walter published the first edition of the *Daily Universal Register*, priced at 2½d.

———•◆•———

1972: Ziggy Stardust, aka David Bowie, was photographed on this day by the photographer Brian Ward, in front of No. 23 Heddon Street W1, creating one of the most celebrated album covers of all time. (*Evening Standard*)

JANUARY 14TH

1437: The pier on which stood the great stone gate of London Bridge collapsed, bringing down the arches on either side. (City of London Records Office)

1896: Birt Acres, a Fellow of the Royal Photographic Society, demonstrated his *Kineopticon* system to members and wives of the Society, at the Queen's Hall in London. This was the first public film show to an audience in the United Kingdom. Robert Paul's first solo theatrical programme was at the Alhambra Theatre on 25 March 1896. (Royal Photographic Society and *The Stage*)

1975: Ian Patching and Paul Charlton were both convicted on this day of posing as plain-clothes policemen when their car overtook Mr Denham's, forced it to stop, then forced Mr Denham into their car, relieved him of his possessions and his clothes and left him naked on Wimbledon Common. They were sentenced to five years. (*Daily Mail*)

January 15th

1867: One of Regent's Park's lakes, frozen over in the winter frosts, gave way as skaters enjoyed themselves. Of the 200 who fell in, forty died. (*The Times*)

———•◆•———

1759: The British Museum, largely based on the collections of the physician and scientist Sir Hans Sloane, first opened to the public on this day in Montagu House in Bloomsbury, on the site of the current museum building. It expanded in the next two and a half years, resulting in the creation of several branches, the first being the British Museum (Natural History) in South Kensington in 1887. Until 1997, when the British Library (previously centered on the Round Reading Room) moved to a new site, the British Museum was unique in that it housed both a national museum of antiquities and a national library in the same building.

———•◆•———

1880: The first telephone directory was published with over 255 names covering three London exchanges.

———•◆•———

1987: The policeman who shot Cherry Groce, an action that sparked off the 1985 riots, was cleared of all criminal charges on this day. (*The Times*)

JANUARY 16TH

1538: The Abbey of St Peter, now known as the Abbey of Westminster, was surrendered to Henry VIII by Abbot Boston and twenty-four of the monks, and the monastery was dissolved.

———•◆•———

1581: On this day Parliament outlawed Catholicism.

———•◆•———

1661: King Charles II appointed Henry Bishop as the first Postmaster General. Bishop was the first to use postmarks.

———•◆•———

1668: Politician, diplomat, gambler, chemist, Satanist, murderer and adulterer George Duke of Buckingham took a mistress, Anna Brudenell, Countess of Shrewsbury. The offended Earl issued a challenge. On this day the two met at Barn Elms, Lady Shrewsbury holding the Duke's horse. Buckingham ran through the Earl, killing him. Pepys would say, 'This will make the world think that the King hath good counselors about him, when the duke of Buckingham, the greatest man about him, is a fellow of no more sobriety than to fight about a whore'.

———•◆•———

1890: On this day Ernest Parke, editor of the *North London Press*, was found guilty of libel. His weekly newspaper was the first to name names in 'The Cleveland Street Scandal'. (*The Times*)

January 17th

1712: Robert Walpole, England's first 'Prime Minister', was imprisoned in the Tower of London following charges of corruption.

———•◆•———

1934: *The Times* reported that Battersea Power Station was fully operational. This was what is known as Battersea A, the initial power station, with an Art Deco interior by Halliday. The second power station, Battersea B, was started in 1944, the fourth chimney not being raised until 1955. The decaying hide of this iconic industrial London landmark has yet to find a suitable and viable new use.

———•◆•———

1983: The BBC fronted its first Breakfast TV programme fronted by Frank Bough and Selina Scott.

———•◆•———

2008: British Airways flight 38 crash-landed just short of London airport with no fatalities, the first complete hull loss of a Boeing 777. (*Daily Mail*)

JANUARY 18TH

1486: The first Tudor King, Henry VII, married Elizabeth of York, the eldest daughter of Edward IV, at Westminster. The Tudor Rose, a combination of the White Rose of York and the Red Rose of Lancaster, became a symbol of their union.

1671: The diplomat and diarist John Evelyn discovered the woodcarver Grinling Gibbons living in a small thatched cottage in Deptford. (*John Evelyn's Diary*)

1738: On this day the law went to the gallows when attorney Thomas Carr was hanged for robbing a William Quarrington of a diamond ring and 93 guineas near Fleet Street. (*Newgate Calendar*)

1989: Raymond Jones, a thirty-one-year-old who killed Miss Yawson, a student, in a savage and motiveless knife attack on a tube between Brixton and Stockwell on 12 December 1987, was jailed for life. (*Daily Mail*)

January 19th

1649: The Puritan Parliament began the trial of Charles I for treason. Charles refused to plead because he did not recognise the legality of the court.

———◆———

1917: Seventy-three people died, including fourteen workers, and more than 400 were injured in a TNT explosion at the Brunner-Mond munitions factory in Silverton. Much of the area was flattened and the shock wave was felt throughout the City and much of Essex. It was the largest explosion in London history and was heard as far as Southampton. (*Daily Mail*)

———◆———

1937: *The Underground Murder Mystery*, a play by J. Bissell Thomas, was the first play to be broadcast by the BBC. It was set in Tottenham Court Road tube station. (BBC)

January 20th

1265: England's first Parliament was convened today by Simon de Montfort and assembled at Westminster Hall.

1649: King Charles I was charged with high treason.

1802: On this day Joseph Wall, ex-governor of an African colony, appeared in court charged with deliberately murdering a subordinate by having him tied to a gun carriage and ordering him to receive 800 lashes, from which he died. He was found guilty and hanged on 29 January. (*Gentleman's Magazine*)

1989: Sir Ranulph Fiennes, the explorer, test-paddled a floating sledge on the Thames by Westminster on the eve of setting off on his third attempt to claim the final unconquered Polar record – a 425-nautical-mile trek to the North Pole without dogs, motorised transport or air supply. (*The Times*)

January 21st

1670: Claude Duval, the 'Gallant Highwayman', was captured at Mother Maberley's tavern, the Hole-in-the-Wall in Chandos Street, when he was drunk and sent to Newgate, where he was tried by Judge Sir William Morton. Despite frantic efforts by the ladies of the Court, and even Charles II himself, Sir William refused to change the sentence of death. The King wished to give a reprieve, but Morton was adamant and, backed by the Judge's threat of resignation, the King gave way. He was hanged on this day and was buried in St Paul's, Covent Garden. (*Newgate Calendar*)

———◆———

1809: St James' Palace caught fire on this day, destroying part of the palace, including the monarch's private apartments at the south-east corner. Over £100,000 worth of damage was caused.

———◆———

2006: A juvenile bottlenose whale was seen swimming in the Thames on 19 January 2006. She was beached near Albert Bridge on this day and efforts were made to transfer her back to sea – unfortunately the whale died in transit. (*Guardian*)

January 22nd

1782: The *Daily Advertiser* recorded the arrival on a cold, rainy and windy day of a distinguished American and his wife, Brigadier-General Benedict Arnold, the most experienced, enterprising, tactical commander America had in their War of Independence.

———◆———

1922: The very young composer William Walton, living at the Sitwell family house at No. 2 Carlyle Square, Chelsea, conducted the first performance of his work *Façade* here, with Edith Sitwell as reciter.

———◆———

1970: Heathrow welcomed the first Jumbo Jet, a Boeing 747 Pan Am, which touched down at 2.14 p.m., seven hours late due to a technical fault. (*Daily Mail*)

———◆———

1988: Alexandra Palace was reopened on this day following a very expensive restoration. The Palm Court included dates and palms brought from Alexandria, Egyptian-style obelisks and mock sphinxes. (*Daily Mail*)

JANUARY 23RD

1571: The first Royal Exchange was opened by Queen Elizabeth: 'The Queen's Majestie attended with her nobility, came from her house at the strande, called Somerset House, and entered the City by Temple-bar, through Fleet streete, Cheap, and so by the north side of the Burse, to Sir Thomas Gresham's where she dined'. (Stow)

———◆———

1903: Mr Justice Wills passed sentence on Arthur Lynch, MP for Galway. Lynch was an Australian–Irish man who had organised Boer farmers in the Boer War. He was eventually accused of adhering to and comforting the King's enemies in South Africa, which was high treason. He was sentenced to hanging, was commuted to life imprisonment, then paroled and had an illustrious career. (*The Times*)

———◆———

1909: Two armed Latvian immigrants snatched the wages from a factory on the corner of Tottenham High Road and Chesnut Road. While trying to escape, they shot and killed PC William Tyler and ten-year-old Ralph Joscelyne. Both robbers shot themselves. (The Tottenham Outrage)

January 24th

1679: Charles II dissolved the 'Long Parliament', an overwhelmingly Royalist parliament that passed, amongst others, the 'Corporation Act', the first of a series of acts to cement the Anglican Church as the official Church of England.

———◆———

1907: William Whiteley, the flamboyant owner of Whiteleys, was shot dead in his office by Horace Raynor who claimed he was his illegitimate son. In view of the claim by the young man's aunt that she had been Whiteley's mistress and had also had a child by him, Raynor's death sentence was commuted to life imprisonment. He was released in 1919 on licence. (*Daily Mail*)

———◆———

1956: Plans were submitted today to build a large complex of residential homes, residential tower blocks, offices and shops in the Barbican area of London, which was very badly bombed area during the war. (*The Times*)

JANUARY 25TH

1731: William Pulteney, MP, leader of the opposition, and Lord Hervey, supporter of the first minister Sir Robert Walpole, fought a duel on Green Park. Pulteney had accused Hervey of being a homosexual. Both men were slightly injured.

1792: The London Corresponding Society, a moderate radical pressure group concentrating on reform of Parliament, was founded today. It was mainly composed of artisans and working men, and had amongst its members the Black Olaudah Equiano.

1839: Henry Fox Talbot showed the photo he had taken of a window at his country home to the Royal Institute in London. He had previously taken several photographic pictures but had never revealed them to anyone. (Royal Photographic Society)

1885: Tobias Simpson died of exhaustion after saving many lives from the breaking ice at Highgate Ponds. (Postman's Park)

1993: The Chelsea & Westminster Hospital in Fulham Road, on the site of the old St Stephen's Hospital, was opened today. Its glass roof is the size of Wembley Stadium. (*Evening Standard*)

JANUARY 26TH

1871: The Rugby Football Union was formed today at a meeting of delegates from twenty-two clubs at the Pall Mall Restaurant. Amongst these were the Harlequins, Blackheath, Richmond and Guy's Hospital. (*The Times*)

1922: Vaughan William's *A Pastoral Symphony*, a work largely influenced by his experiences as an ambulance volunteer in the First World War, was premiered today in London, with Adrian Boult conducting. (*The Times*)

1927: Members of the Royal Institution and other visitors to a laboratory in an upper room in Frith Street, Soho, saw a demonstration of an apparatus invented by Mr J.L. Baird, called a televisor. (BBC)

1960: Michael Black, aged thirty-one, a company director with assets of about £30,000, was sentenced to fifteen months' imprisonment after pleading guilty to burglary at a house in Acacia Road, St John's Wood. He had scaled a 40ft stack pipe, broken into the house and stole jewellry while the alarm rang. The police eventually found him hiding behind a chimney stack. (*The Times*)

January 27th

1796: On this day it was reported that Lady Caroline Campbell 'displayed in Hyde Park the other day a feather four feet higher than her bonnet'. (*Gentleman's Magazine*)

---◆---

1854: On this Friday the Law Courts were still at Westminster and it was proposed that they be re-sited in the Strand: a leading article commented that this would be an idea like 'the Tower of Babel ... A Nero's Palace, A Labyrinth of Crete ... in short a waste of public money'. (*The Times*)

---◆---

1960: The Civil Appropriation Accounts published on this day showed a saving of £7,770 in the salaries and expenses of the House of Commons through MPs declining to take their salaries and one minister deciding to forego a salary of £750. (*The Times*)

---◆---

1975: Monday – an IRA bomb exploded outside Gieves, in Old Bond Street at 9.30 p.m., injuring a security guard. Just before 11 p.m. two men and a woman were injured by a bomb in a jewellers in Kensington High Street, and at 11.35 p.m. another exploded at the Army and Navy Stores in Victoria Street, slightly injuring two people. (*Daily Mail*)

JANUARY 28TH

1547: Henry VIII 'dyed at hys most princely howse at Westminster, comenly called Yorkeplace or Whytehall'. (Stow)

1785: On this day Sir Ashton Lever advertised lottery tickets to obtain his famous collection from Leicester House in Leicetser Square at 1 guinea a ticket. (*Gentleman's Magazine*)

1807: Friedrich Albert Winzer, a German entrepreneur living in London, was interested in the properties of gas. He patented coal-gas lighting in 1804 and, on moving into a house in Pall Mall, set up gas lamps that first lit on this day. Pall Mall was the first gas-lit street and remains so. (*The Times*)

1953: Derek Bentley, an educationally disadvantaged youth of twenty who had fatally shot a policeman in a botched burglary in Croydon, was hanged. (*Daily Mail*)

January 29th

1753: Nineteen-year-old Elizabeth Canning reappeared today after having disappeared from her home on 1 January. She claimed she had been kidnapped by a Mary Squires. Squires was tried and sentenced to death but pardoned through lack of evidence. Elizabeth was tried for perjury and sent to the colonies. (*Newgate Calendar*)

1801: Emma Hamilton, lover of Nelson, gave birth to twin daughters at a house on Clarges Street. As she could only cope with one child, she sent the other to a foundling hospital in Holborn. Nelson was told only one survived. He wrote, 'a finer child was never produced by any two persons. In truth a love-begotten child'.

1842: The body of PC Nicholls, 'his face much bruised and disfigured as if from severe violence', was found at 6 a.m. on South Lambeth Road. In 1982, 140 years later, a Kennington policeman investigated this 'death by the visitation of God'. Police records pointed to another officer who found his body. The officer had a grudge, and moreover the relevant page in a police register of the time was missing. (*South London Press*)

JANUARY 30TH

1649: At 2 p.m. King Charles I was decapitated at Whitehall in full view of a large crowd. The only regicide.

1661: 'This day were the carcasses of those arch-rebels, Cromwell, Bradshaw and General Ireton dragged out of their superb tombs in Westminster ... to Tyburn and hanged on the gallows, and then buried in a deep pit.' Their heads were displayed on spikes on the roof of Westminster Hall. (*John Evelyn's Diary*)

1965: The late sir Winston Churchill had a state funeral on this day. His coffin was carried from Westminster Hall, taken to St Paul's, then to Tower Pier and barqued downriver to Waterloo and on to Bladon churchyard. (*The Times*)

1969: The Beatles played their last ever gig on the roof of Apple Records Office at No. 3 Savile Row. The police stopped the performance after forty minutes, following complaints from neighbouring offices. (*Daily Mail*)

JANUARY 31ST

1825: The nineteen-year-old flower seller Maria Briscolie was found dead on the floor of her room, her stomach filed with laudanum. She had committed suicide because she had been abandoned by her rich lover when her baby died. (*Examiner*)

1867: Nelson's Testimonial Committee had included four lions at the corners of Nelson's Column. The lions were to be in stone or granite … this idea was contentious. Lack of funding and artistic arguments prevented any way forward. Funds became available in 1846 to commission these at the base of the column. In 1858 Parliament allocated £6,000 for the completion of the lions and the intent was to invite six sculptors to submit models and for one of them to be selected. This caused controversy. Sir Edwin Landseer was then proposed; this caused even more raised eyebrows. Finally the sculptor Baron Carlo Marochetti was asked to sculpt them in bronze and on this day his lions were unveiled in Trafalgar Square. *Reynolds's Weekly Newspaper* said, 'although admirable in most respects they have certainly some glaring defects.' The consensus of opinion was that they looked more like sphinxes than lions. (*The Times*)

FEBRUARY 1ST

1444: On this day lightning hit and set fire to the steeple of St Paul's. It was eventually put out by Londoners. (Stow)

1814: The last Frost Fair started today and lasted four days. An elephant was led across the river at Blackfriars Bridge. (*The Times*)

1815: Joanna Southcott, a religious fanatic, died today. By this time she had a following of 140,000 and claimed she was pregnant. An autopsy showed that she was not. The spirit of her 'phantom' child Shiloh is believed by modern Southcottians to reside in Prince William.

1971: Karpal Kaur Sandhu, born in Zanzibar, but of Indian parentage, became Britain's and the Met's first female Asian police officer. Unfortunately her husband murdered her in 1973 because he thought her career was neither Asian nor ladylike. (*Walthamstow Guardian*)

February 2nd

1255: An African elephant presented to Henry III by King Louis IX of France joined the Royal menagerie at the Tower of London on this day – it died in 1258 of a surfeit of red wine. (*Baker's Chronicle*)

————◆————

1626: On this day Charles I was crowned. His Catholic queen refused to attend and there was no procession. The royal barge, furthermore, fouled the landing stage and ran aground at Parliament Stairs so that the King had to come ashore in another boat.

————◆————

1852: The first public toilets were opened at No. 95 Fleet Street today. These 'Public Waiting Rooms' were advertised in *The Times*.

————◆————

1880: The first shipment of frozen meat from Australia arrived in London in excellent condition. (*The Times*)

————◆————

1988: On this Tuesday evening a group of lesbians abseiled from the visitors' gallery in the House of Lords in protest at the ban on the promotion of homosexuality. They had been allowed in on the cognisance of Lord Monkswell – he issued an apology a few days later. (*Daily Mail*)

FEBRUARY 3RD

1730: The first Stock Exchange quotations were published in the *Advertiser* today.

———◆———

1813: John and Leigh Hunt, brother proprietors of the *Examiner*, were imprisoned for seditious libel against the Prince Regent on this day. They had printed that he was 'the disappointer of hopes' and that this 'Adonis in loveliness' was 'a corpulent gentleman of fifty, a violator of his word, a libertine, over head and ears in debt and a disgrace'.

———◆———

1814: A piece of ice broke off and floated free at a Frost Fair, just above Westminster Bridge, with two youths on it. One slipped, the action titled both into the water and they died. (*Examiner*)

———◆———

1975: On this day Eduardo Gatica, a Chilean pickpocket gang leader who had entered Britain with a false passport, was found guilty of attempted theft, along with several accomplices, at Victoria Coach Station. (*Daily Mail*)

———◆———

1975: On the same day Prince Charles was called to the Bar at Gray's Inn and became Master of the Bench. (*The Times*)

February 4th

1748: Jeremy Bentham, future jurist, philosopher and legal and social reformer, was born on this day at Church Lane, Houndsditch. (*Oxford Dictionary of National Biography*)

———◆———

1962: *The Sunday Times* published '*The Sunday Times* colour section' today – the first newspaper colour supplement in the UK.

———◆———

1973: The first processional lion danced through the streets of Soho as part of the Chinese New Year on this day. The organisers had decided to show that there were now many Chinese in London and that this area was now Chinatown. It had previously been in the East End. (*Daily Telegraph*)

———◆———

1975: Builders working in the London headquarters of the Communist Party in King Street, Covent Garden, found a bugging device in a panel on the dais. It had a range of 50m and had been installed about ten years previously. (*The Times*)

———◆———

1975: On the same day Fire Brigade ladders were too short to save Roy Field from a blaze on the thirteenth floor of Longlents House, Shrewsbury Crescent, Willesden. (*Willesden Herald*)

FEBRUARY 5TH

1974: An IRA bomb was placed at the Earl's Court Show and everyone had to be evacuated. (*Daily Mail*)

—◆—

1969: Reginald Kray, on trial with his brother Ronald at the Old Bailey for the murder of Jack McVitie in 1967, interrupted the trial to call the Crown Counsel a 'fat slob' and the police 'animals and fat slobs'. (*Daily Mail*)

—◆—

1969: After the Ronan Point tragedy, new building regulations were introduced. As a consequence a twelve-storey block of flats, Burghley Tower, in Acton, was declared unsafe on this day. The tenants would be found alternate temporary accommodation while the block was strengthened. (*The Times*)

—◆—

1983: A Dyno-Rod engineer called out to deal with a blocked drain outside No. 23 Cranley Gardens, Muswell Hill, thought the blockage looked suspiciously like human flesh. By the next day police had visited Dennis Nilsen at the address. He calmly told them that he had butchered fifteen or sixteen people since 1978. (*Sunday Times*)

FEBRUARY 6TH

1969: A special squad of detectives was set up in Barnes on this day to investigate thefts of parking-meter boxes after several hundred empty ones were found in the Thames. (*Daily Mail*)

———•◆•———

1969: Shopfitters had been putting in a new shop front to Mappin and Webb Jewellers in Brompton Road. On this day three men arrived with a hardboard screen and erected it inside, working behind it. They left a couple of hours later. It was only much later in the afternoon that a customer pointed out that the window display was empty and that there was a hole in the plate glass. The 'workmen' had calmly stolen jewellery worth £10,000 while staff were dealing with customers. (*Daily Mail*)

———•◆•———

1975: Today two emaciated Romanian stowaways were rescued by London dockers from a Romanian ship at the Port of London while the crew was kept busy in an immigration check. Once ashore two Romanian officers tried to intervene, but a group of dockers formed a protective circle around the two until ambulances arrived. (*Daily Mail*)

FEBRUARY 7TH

1729: On this day *Bradley's Weekly Messenger* reported that a fire extinguisher, patented by Ambrose Godfrey Hauckwitz, was used to put out a fire in London.

1845: Late on this Friday afternoon a young William Lloyd threw a chunk of granite and smashed the priceless 'Portland Vase' in the British Museum. He admitted in Court that he had been drunk for most of the week. Although the vase was priceless, he could only be charged £3 for smashing the glass case. (*The Times*)

1907: On this Thursday more than 3,000 members and supporters of the National Union of Women's Suffrage, led by Lady Strachey, Millicent Fawcett, Lady Frances Balfour and Keir Hardie, marched through the damp and cold streets of London, from Hyde Park to Exeter Hall. Their objective was to force through votes for women in a non-militant activity. It became known as the 'Mud March'. (*The Mail*)

1974: Following the announcement of the miner's strike, the Prime Minister Edward Heath called a general election. Harold Wilson won. (*The Times*)

FEBRUARY 8TH

1976: Joan Bazely became the first woman to referee a football match today; it was between two men's teams at Croydon. (*Croydon Advertiser*)

———◆———

1750: On this day slight damage and much consternation was caused by a tremor in London. A more powerful tremor on 8 March caused even more apprehension – what would happen on 8 April? Thousands of Londoners slept on London's northern hills – but nothing happened. (*Gentleman's Magazine*)

———◆———

1671: Richard Penderel, a yeoman farmer who had helped Charles II escape the disastrous defeat at the Battle of Worcester in 1651, hiding him in local woods and assisting his departure, died in London on this day and was buried in St Giles-in-the-Fields. His tomb was annually decorated with oak branches. (Registers)

———◆———

1804: Mathesulah Spalding was hanged outside Newgate on this cold winter's day 'for an unnatural crime, a deed without a name … nature shudders at it'! (*Newgate Calendar*)

———◆———

1888: A bitterly cold winter and the support of radical groups led to a rally of 20,000 disaffected men in Trafalgar Square today. The protest turned violent at Pall Mall in the Carlton Club where a clubman was seen holding his nose in disgust. All the Club windows were smashed as well as there being general chaos. (*The Times*)

FEBRUARY 9TH

1791: The Annual Registry recorded that the Thames rose to 'an amazing height … New Palace Yard and Westminster Hall were overflowed and the lawyers were conveyed to and from the courts in boats. The water rose through the sewers and overflowed the privy gardens … and the damage done in the warehouses on the wharfs on both on both sides of the river is immense …'

————◆————

1792: Johann Jakob Schweppe, a German Swiss, arrived in London on this day to start a factory making seltzer water. The first factory was at No. 141 Drury Lane. Despite his business flat lining and his Swiss partners dissolving the partnership, Mr Schweppe persevered and was patroned by Erasmus Darwin. 'Soda Water' was coined in the same decade and has never gone flat since! (*The Times*)

————◆————

1996: An IRA seventeen-month ceasefire was dramatically broken by a 500kg bomb in a truck exploding at South Quay, Canary Wharf, at 7 p.m. Two people were killed and thirty-nine required hospital treatment. Over £100 million worth of damage was caused. (*Daily Mail*)

FEBRUARY 10TH

1746: Mr Pelham's administration resigned en masse. King George I turned to Pulteney, Earl of Bath on this day to form an alternative ministry. He accepted the Seals of Office and made nominations, but did not have enough support to form a viable government, and after forty-eight hours, three quarters, seven minutes and eleven seconds, he abandoned the attempt forcing the King to accept Pelham's demands. (Horace Walpole: letter to Sir Horace Mann)

1840: Queen Victoria married her first cousin Prince Albert of Saxe-Coburg-Gotha in the Chapel Royal of St James's Palace on this day. She proposed to her future husband despite telling Lord Melbourne beforehand that marriage was 'a shocking alternative' to living with her mother.

1971: The *Guardian* reported that Frank Zappa was banned from appearing at The Albert Hall because the management protested at the lyrics of his new Rock Opera *Two Hundred Motels*. He brought an action against them but the initial ruling was upheld in 1975.

FEBRUARY 11TH

1826: London University, later University College London, was granted its Charter on this day. It was the first London university and the first English university to be established on a secular basis, to admit women on equal terms with men and to 'admit students regardless of religion.'

———◆———

1862: On this day Elizabeth Siddal, wife of Dante Gabriel Rossetti, died of an overdose. The grief-stricken Rossetti placed his notebook in her coffin. She was buried in Highgate and exhumed seven years later so that Rossetti could retrieve his notebook. Her body was said to have no trace of decomposition. (*Oxford Dictionary of National Biography*)

———◆———

1966: On this Friday the House of Commons voted 164-107 for the Reform of the Homosexual Law in light of the Wolfenden Report eight years previously. One MP, Leo Abse, said that it was as ludicrous to send a homosexual to a male prison as it was sending a sex maniac to a harem. (*The Times*)

———◆———

1981: Iftikhar Ahmed, of Forest Gate, working for the ILEA, complained to the European Commission of Human Rights that the British government contravened his human rights by denying him time off with pay to attend mosque on Fridays. (*The Times*)

February 12th

1424: The royal prisoner James I of Scotland married Jane Beaufort at St Mary Overie, Southwark, on this day.

---•◆•---

1832: Sarah Ferguson of White's Rents, Nightingale Lane, was taken ill then moved to Limehouse Workhouse where she died eight hours later. Her extremities turned blue shortly before her death, confirming her ailment as being Asiatic cholera. (*The Times*)

---•◆•---

1682: Thomas Thynne, master of Longleat, was shot dead in his coach outside what is now the Institute of Directors, on this evening. The killers, Capt. Vratz, Lt Stern and a Pole called Boroski, hired by Count Konigsmarck, were hunted down and executed. Not the Count, however. He had arranged this because he coveted Thynne's wife. (*Oxford Dictionary of National Biography*)

---•◆•---

1990: The Savoy Theatre's auditorium was ravaged by fire in the early hours. It was recreated in its original mould and reopened on 19 July 1993. (*The Times*)

FEBRUARY 13TH

1247: 'There happened a dreadfulle earthquake which threw downe many of the houses of the City of London, and occasioned other considerable damage.' (*History of London*, Henry Chamberlain, 1770)

—————•◆•—————

1897: On this Saturday at Lambeth Court, Ada Bennett, aged forty-five, a midwife of King's Road, Peckham, was charged on remand before Mr Denman, with performing an illegal operation on one Eleanor Cook. The defendant's counsel, Mr W.H. Armstrong, apologised for the various delays and proposed to retire from the case due to his client's dissatisfaction with him. (Police Report)

—————•◆•—————

1907: The King's speech had not mentioned giving women the vote, so on this day the Pankhursts and Charlotte Despard organised 400 women to march to Parliament. They were stopped by massed police outside Westminster Abbey where scuffles broke out. Sixty women were arrested but several managed to go to the lobby of the Houses of Parliament. (*The Times*)

FEBRUARY 14TH

1752: On a whim, the Duke of Hamilton married the socialite Elizabeth Gunning at the Mayfair Chapel. The lack of a gold band meant that an old brass washer had to be used. Along with her sibling, Elizabeth was one of the most beautiful young women of her time.

———◆———

1895: Oscar Wilde's play, *The Importance of Being Earnest*, was premiered at the St James Theatre Its high farce and witty dialogue has helped make it Wilde's most enduringly popular play.

———◆———

1852: The Hospital for Sick Children (The Great Ormond Street Hospital for Children) was founded today. It was the first hospital providing in-patient care especially for children in the English-speaking world. (*The Times*)

———◆———

1946: The Bank of England Act 1946 nationalised the Bank of England on this day.

———◆———

1997: On this day jurors at the inquest of Stephen Lawrence, the eighteen-year-old black youth killed at a bus stop in Eltham in 1993, decided that he was killed unlawfully in a completely unprovoked racist attack by white youths. (*Guardian*)

February 15th

1894: The anarchist Martin Bourdin was killed by his own bomb near the Royal Observatory, Greenwich Park. He was identified by his Autonomie Club membership card. Police raided his lodgings at No. 18 Great Titchfield Street where they found sulphuric acid. (*The Times*)

1759: Montague House became the repository for Sir Hans Sloane's cabinet of 70,000 curiosities he had bequeathed to the nation – this became the hub of the British Museum.

2003: On this day two huge columns of protestors, one from the Embankment, the other from Gower Street, converged at Piccadilly and continued to Hyde Park for a rally against the impending war on Iraq. Opinions vary on the numbers involved; the police said 750,000, the BBC 1 million and the organisers 2 million. (*Guardian*)

FEBRUARY 16TH

1587: On this day Sir Philip Sidney, soldier statesman and poet, who had died in October 1586, was given a public funeral. He was memorialised as the flower of English manhood in Edmund Spenser's 'Astrophel'. (Thomas Lant)

———◆———

1978: On this Friday George Davis, an East End mini-cab driver, was cleared in the Crown Court of taking part in a £47,000 whisky raid five years previously, but was remanded in custody to face trial on a charge concerning a £50,000 London Bank raid for which he was convicted. (*The Times*)

———◆———

1824: On this day John Wilson Croker convened a meeting of scientists and friends, such as Sir Thomas Lawrence and Sir Whitelaw Ainslie, to establish a 'club for scientific and literary men and artists', the Athenaeum. He is credited with coining the political description of 'Conservative'. (*Oxford Dictionary of National Biography*)

———◆———

1989: Dr Raymond Crockett, a Harley Street nephrologist and director of the National Kidney Centre, resigned this latter post on this day after revelations that kidneys had been purchased from impoverished Turks to be used in transplants for wealthy patients at the Wellington Humana Hospital. He was struck off by the GMC. (*Journal of Medical Ethics*)

February 17th

1872: At 2 a.m on this Saturday, George Merrett, a father of six, was shot dead outside his place of work, the Red Lion Brewery, SE1. His killer, a deranged American doctor, was one William Chester Minor. He was certified insane on 6 April and spent the rest of his long life in Broadmoor Prison, contributing heavily to the *New Oxford Dictionary*.

———◆———

1726: On this Sunday César de Saussure, a Swiss nobleman, had his pocket picked of a valuable snuff box in a small street leading into St James' Park. (*Lettres d'Angleterre*, C. de Saussure)

———◆———

1932: On this Wednesday, the Twit Club, No. 18 Piccadilly, was advertised as being open to any gentleman 'wishing to 'partake in the delights of the Capital'. Members to contact were Mr Cyril Fairman, Mr Anthony Beresford or Louis Count de Loriol c/o Martin's Bank St James Square, W1. (*Daily Telegraph*)

FEBRUARY 18TH

1478: Richard Duke of Gloucester is said to have ordered his brother George Duke of Clarence's execution – he was drowned in a butt of Malmsey wine in the Tower of London on this day. (*Chambers Book of Days*, 1854)

1795: Hyder, 'a Black servant boy, native of Bengal, aged 14' absconded from No. 58 Baker Street, Portman Square, where he was employed. (*Morning Chronicle*)

1709: Joseph Billers, silkman and thief-taker, of Cheapside, established his innocence before Chief-Justice Holt at the Guildhall when charged maliciously and falsely of corruptly attempting to obtain a reprieve for John Read, a horse-thief. Corrupt City officials had also been involved. (City of London Records Office)

1919: The first prototype 3-litre model Bentley car was finished today at W.O. Bentley's workshop in New Street Mews, off Baker Street. (*London Plaques*)

1901: The new MP Winston Churchill made his maiden speech in the House of Commons today. He tried to justify the burning of Boer farms during the war on the basis of precedent and rational warfare. (Hansard)

February 19th

1982: *The South London Press* noted today that Brixton police had adopted identity parades taken in busy underground stations where suspects mingled freely with the crowd at the foot of the escalators, whilst the witness was at the top looking at the crowd. This method of identification was used for ethnic minorities as they were reluctant to come to formal identity parades.

————•◆•————

1925: John Barrymore, the American actor, decided to play Hamlet in London but no one would back him. He therefore financed his own production which opened today at the Haymarket Theatre. His performance was rated 'magnificent' and he made a profit of £10, 000. (*Variety*)

————•◆•————

1978: On this Sunday about 250 demonstrators marched through London to mark the first anniversary of the arrest, under the Official Secrets Act, of Crispin Aubrey, a journalist, John Berry, a former soldier, and Duncan Campbell, a writer. Berry had been charged with communicating classified information to unauthorised persons. The ensuing ABC trial provoked even more controversy. (The Associated Press)

FEBRUARY 20TH

1547: The nine-year-old King Edward VI (1537-53) was crowned at Westminster Abbey on this day. One unusual feature of the procession to the abbey was a Spaniard who descended from a rope from the battlements of St Paul's steeple fastened to an anchor near the gate of the Deanery. (Stow)

1913: Suffragettes had to resort to desperate measures to publicise their cause – a group of them set fire to the Tea Pavilion in Kew on this day. The constables gave chase, and just before they caught them each of the women who had separated was seen to throw away a portmanteau. At the station the women gave the names of Lilian Lenton and Olive Wharry. 'In one of the bags which the women threw away were found a hammer, a saw, a bundle to tow, strongly redolent of paraffin and some paper smelling strongly of tar. The other bag was empty, but it had evidently contained inflammables.' (Old Bailey Records)

1965: This Sunday a man walked into the Brompton Oratory Roman Catholic church in the afternoon and walked out at about 4 p.m. with the 'Ghost chair', a crimson backed hardwood chair found in a ruined church in south America and brought back by Colonel Fawcett, the explorer. (*Daily Mail*)

FEBRUARY 21ST

1702: William III's horse stumbled on a molehill at Hampton Court Park on this day, throwing his charge. The King broke his collar bone, and died on 8 March. The Jacobites would raise a toast to the 'Little Gentleman in Velvet' who did this deed.

1803: Lt-Col. Edward Marcus Despard was hanged for treason on this day. He was alleged to have plotted to assassinate the King and seize the Tower. He remained silent during his trial. Despite an appeal for clemency, he was hanged and then decapitated. The executioner then held up his head, shouting, 'This is the head of a traitor'. (*Newgate Calendar*)

1867: The Memorial Tablet Committee at the Society of Arts on this day had a difference of opinion over the first plaque to be erected in London. Nelson was to have been the first to be so honoured – instead Napoleon III would have one! (Society of Arts Minutes)

1934: Giro, the German ambassador Leopold von Hoesch's dog, was accidentally electrocuted on this day. He was given a full Nazi burial in the Embassy Garden at No. 9 Carlton House Terrace, WI. (*The Times*)

FEBRUARY 22ND

1838: Jane Alsop, an eighteen-year-old living between Bow and Old Ford, answered a ringing at the gate and was confronted by a man in a cloak claiming to be a policeman. He called out, 'For God's sake, bring me a light for we have caught Spring-heeled Jack herein the lane'. She fetched a candle and he immediately revealed himself, vomiting blue and white flame, his eyes red balls of fire. She and her sister fought him off. (*The Times*)

———•◦•———

1864: The last execution of a group of prisoners outside Newgate Jail took place on this day when five men named Blanco, Leone, Duranno, Lopez and Watts were hanged for the murder of the captain of the ship *Flowery Land*. (*Newgate Calendar*)

———•◦•———

1897: Jean-François Gravelet (1824–1897), better known as the acrobat 'Blondin', died of diabetes at Niagara House in Northfields this Monday. He was buried in Kensal Green. (Kensal Green cemetery)

FEBRUARY 23RD

1732: Handel's *Oratorio* was performed for the first time at the Crown & Anchor Tavern, London, on the composer's forty-seventh birthday, and was the first oratorio ever performed in Britain.

————◆————

1820: The Cato Street conspiracy to assassinate the British Cabinet and Prime Minister Castlereagh was uncovered. It was planned by Arthur Thistlewood in a house in Cato Street, off Edgware Road, London, where he was arrested. Found guilty, he was imprisoned in the Tower (the last prisoner ever held there), before being executed with other accomplices in May.

————◆————

1944: During a bombing raid, the St James' Palace clock was destroyed, King Street was transformed into a river of fire and the London Library was hit.

FEBRUARY 24TH

1711: The first Italian opera, *Rinaldo* by G.F. Handel, written for the London stage, premiered at the Queen's Theatre in the Haymarket.

———•———

1857: Buckingham Palace announced that sixty-two veterans of the Crimean War would be the first-ever recipients of the Victoria Cross – these were crafted from the Russian guns seized at Sebastopol. (*The Times*)

———•———

1920: Nancy Astor, 1879–1964, the first woman MP to sit in the House of Commons, made her maiden speech today, making her the first woman to speak in Parliament.

———•———

1981: Ending months of speculation, Buckingham Palace announced that Prince Charles, the heir to the throne, would marry Lady Diana Spencer. (BBC)

———•———

1988: The first baby born from an embryo after the fertilisation of a donated egg was delivered at Dulwich Hospital by Caesarean section. (BBC)

FEBRUARY 25TH

1822: The first body for dissection was received at a house in Hosier Lane. It was the body of William Abott, hanged at Newgate for the murder of May Lees. (*Newgate Calendar*)

———•◆•———

1824: On this day Sir John Wrottesley introduced a debate on the metric system in Parliament. The metric system was, by that time, widely used in Europe and he believed a uniform metric system would benefit the economy. (*The Times*)

———•◆•———

1838: At about 8 p.m. there was a knock at the door of No. 2 Turner Street, Whitechapel. A servant answered the door to a tall shadowy caped figure. The figure threw its cloak, revealing a hideous face, and then bounded off when the servant cried for help. (*Morning Chronicle*)

———•◆•———

1899: The first driver to die in a car accident was Edwin Sewell, who was test driving a 6hp Daimler down Grove Hill, Harrow, when the rear wheels collapsed. Damages of £655 were awarded against the company. (Daimler Archives)

FEBRUARY 26TH

1717: On this Wednesday the nineteen-year-old French army captain, Gilbert Motier, Marquis de Lafayette, future antagonist of the British armies in the Americas, paid a visit to Lord Stormont in London. He was introduced to King George III at a levee the following day.

1797: Faced with the shortage of gold, due in great part to the wars in Europe and America, the Bank of England issued the first £1 note, printed on one side only. (*Bank of England*)

2004: The first British citizenship ceremony was held in Brent. Nineteen immigrants swore an 'Oath of Allegiance to the Queen' and 'pledged to uphold British Democratic Values'. (LB Brent)

FEBRUARY 27TH

1557: The first Russian Embassy opened in London today. Exactly a year later a trade mission from Russia reached London, bringing many sable skins. (Henry Machyn)

1770: 'Tonight, Monday, near 800 of the nobility and Gentry attended a masked ball at Carlisle House, Mrs Cornely's home ... the richness and brilliancy of the dresses was almost beyond imagination ... at six in the morning three or four hundred remained in the rooms.' (*General Evening Post*)

1900: The Labour party was founded in London on this day, by combining the Independent Labour party, the Fabian Society and the Trade Union movement; Ramsay Macdonald was its first secretary.

1907: The Old Bailey, named because it is sited on a street of that name, but properly called the Central Criminal Court, was officially opened today. Ironically it also stands on the site of the Old Court Prison, Newgate. (City of London Records Office)

FEBRUARY 28TH

1838: At 8.30 p.m., Lucy Scales, the sister of a Limehouse butcher, was walking along a narrow street with her younger sister when they were confronted by a tall, thin figure cloaked in black. He spat blue flame, fumed into her face, then turned hard and left 'with extreme speed'. Both sisters described the events identically. (*The Times*)

1874: Arthur Orton, an Australian, was today sentenced to fourteen years' imprisonment with hard labour for 'falsely swearing he was Roger Charles Tichborne, that he seduced Catherine Doughty in 1871 and that he was not Arthur Orton'. This was the longest trial up until then in England. (*The Times*)

1948: King George VI, his queen, two daughters and the Duke of Edinburgh, went to see Danny Kaye at the London Palladium, the first non-command performance attended by a reigning monarch. (*Daily Mail*)

1975: An underground train crashed at Moorgate tube station, killing thirty people and seriously injuring more than fifty. (*Daily Mail*)

1989: The world's largest litter bin was placed in Covent Garden on this day, sponsored by Kentucky Fried Chicken. (*Sun*)

FEBRUARY 29TH

1928: On this day Police-Sgt George Goddard, stationed at Vine Street, was convicted of accepting large sums of money from nightclub owners for protecting them from and warning them of police raids. He had also stashed at least £12, 000 away in bank accounts. He asked for his money to be returned as it was not part of the ongoing investigation. (*The Times*)

———•◆•———

1928: Harry Craddock, barman of the Savoy Hotel, created the 'leap-year cocktail' for the leap-year celebrations at the Savoy. The ingredients were 2 shots of Bombay dry London gin, ½ shot Grand Marnier liqueur, ½ shot Martini Rosso sweet vermouth, and ¼ shot freshly squeezed lemon juice – the instructions were to shake and serve in a chilled cocktail glass. (*1930 Savoy Cocktail Book*)

———•◆•———

1860: George Bridgetower, a musical prodigy and violinist, died on this day in Peckham. Of mixed race, he was born to a Barbadian servant of Prince Radziwill and his Polish wife, in Poland. He and his father had moved to Britain by 1790, where he came under the protection of the Prince of Wales. He was to have a very successful career in Britain. (*The Times*)

MARCH 1ST

1912: The Women's Social & Political Union had always announced militant demonstrations well in advance. On this day, for the for the first time, the Union struck without warning: about 150 women were given hammers, told exactly which windows to break, when to break them, and how to hit panes low so that glass would not fall from above. At 5.45 p.m. in Oxford Street, Regent Street, the Strand, and other prominent thoroughfares, well-dressed women produced hammers from handbags and began to smash windows. The firms whose windows were damaged included Burberry, Liberty, Marshall & Snelgrove, and Kodak. Foreign firms were not exempt: windows were broken at the offices of the Canadian Pacific, the Grand Trunk Railway, and Norddeutscher Lloyd. The damage was estimated at £5,000. Police arrested 124 women. (*The Times*)

1711: The first issue of the *Spectator*, founded by Joseph Addison and Richard Steele, was published today.

MARCH 2ND

1717: Dancing Master John Weaver experimented with a new form of entertainment by eliminating words and trying to convey dramatic action through dance and pantomime. On this day he had performed the first ballet in England at Drury Lane, the 'Loves of Mars and Venus'.

1826: *The Times* reported that the elephant named Chunee, kept at Edward Cross's menagerie at the old Exeter Exchange in the Strand, went mad, ' … it was destroyed by order of the proprietor … the work of death was accomplished by repeated discharges of musketry, the noise of which … being distinctly heard in the Strand'.

1854: On this day Mr Witham, the magistrate, found Jane Browning of Vere Street guilty of 'unlawfully assaulting, beating and inflicting grievous bodily harm on Harriet Gunton'. He sentenced her to one year's imprisonment with hard labour. She had been pretending to cure Harriet of 'worms', and 'operated' on her, purportedly taking an eel out of her body that was shown in court. (*The Times*)

MARCH 3RD

1415: The year of Agincourt – on this day the convent of the Bridgettine Order was founded in Twickenham. In the Royal Charter it was named 'The Monastery of St Saviour and St Bridget of Syon', and it was first built near where Twickenham Bridge crosses the Thames today. The Order of the Most Holy Saviour, more commonly known as the Bridgettine Order, was founded in 1377 by Queen Brigitta or Bridget of Sweden, the great Swedish mystic who was later canonised. It became one of the richest, most fashionable, and influential religious communities of women in the country until its dissolution under King Henry VIII.

———•◆•———

1943: The Bethnal Green air-raid shelter was the scene of carnage on this day because of panic. A mother carrying a child fell down a flight of stairs, swiftly followed by an elderly man falling on top of her. Lines of people tripped over others as they tried to enter the shelter. In all, 178 people died, including the baby. The mother, however, survived. (*The Times*)

MARCH 4TH

1903: The Adorers of the Sacred Heart of Jesus of Montmartre OSB, led by their founder, Mother Marie Adèle Garnier, had fled to England in 1901. She opened her convent, also known as the Tyburn Nuns, at the site of the martyrdom of more than 100 Catholic Reformation martyrs, No. 8 Hyde Park Place, on this day. (*Catholic Herald*)

————◆◆————

1824: George Hibbert and Sir William Hillary organised a meeting at the Tavern in Bishopsgate Street, which resulted in the establishment of the National Institution for the Preservation of Life from Shipwreck, later to become the Royal National Lifeboat Institution.

————◆◆————

1882: The North Metropolitan Tramways Co. used the short length of horse tramway in Leytonstone High Road extended to the Green Man, to experiment in 1877 with the Merryweather steam tram; in 1881 to experiment with a car driven by the Beaumont compressed air engine; and on this day with an electric tram run on a battery. (*Victoria County Histories*)

MARCH 5TH

1856: The original Covent Garden Theatre was destroyed by fire during a bal masqué held by Mr Anderson, the Wizard of the North. It was rebuilt by Edward Barry and reopened in 1858. (*The Times*)

***

1857: James Townsend Saward, aged fifty-eight, described as a labourer, and James Anderson, aged thirty-six, a servant, were brought to the Central Criminal Court to face charges of forgery. Saward, a solicitor with chambers in the Temple, was also, due to his position in society, described as the most notorious forger of his age, and was known as 'Jim the Penman'. Both were later convicted and sentenced to transportation to a penal colony in Australia. (*The Times*)

***

1879: A coal porter found a large wooden box in the river Thames near Barnes Bridge. Once opened, it was found to contain gelatinous human remains. These were eventually found to be those of Miss Julia Thomas of No. 2 Richmond Terrace – Kate Webster, her servant, was her murderer. A skull recently found in the garden of naturalist David Attenborough, who now resides at the house, may well be hers. (*Great British Trials*)

MARCH 6TH

1997: A Picasso painting, the 'Tête de Femme', worth £700,000, was stolen from the Lefevre Gallery in the West End on this day just after 11 a.m. The thief was a slim pony-tailed man in his early thirties, armed with a sawn-off shot gun. The raid took thirty-five seconds and was captured on video cameras. The thief jumped in a taxi, and was at first taken to Halfords in Battersea where he made a hurried phone call, and then Wimbledon where he disappeared. (*The Times*)

1998: A pensioner from Shirley called the meteorological office in Bracknell in a state of distress after seeing her garden and street covered in dead frogs. (*Croydon Advertiser*)

1998: On this Friday the Union Flag flew at full mast from Buckingham Palace, prompted by the death of Diana, Princess of Wales. The flag will now fly twenty-four hours a day when the Queen is not there. Previously tradition dictated that no flag flew when the Queen was not in residence. (*The Times*)

MARCH 7TH

1733: Sarah Malcolm was hanged near Fetter Lane for the murder of Mrs Duncombe, her employer, Elizabeth Harrison, and Ann Price, her employer's servant, as well as stealing silver and valuables. She admitted to the robbery along with Martha Tracy, and Thomas and James Alexander, but denied the murders. She alone was convicted of both crimes. She was twenty-two. (*Newgate Calendar*)

1804: The Royal Horticultural Society was founded by Sir Joseph Banks and John Wedgwood for the encouragement and improvement of the science, art and practice of horticulture. The first meeting was chaired by John Wedgwood on this day. (RHS)

1895: Frank Taylor, an out-of-work plasterer living at Fountain Road, Tooting, with his wife and seven children, murdered all his family bar one by slitting their throats. He then slit his own throat. One of his children, although badly wounded, managed to raise the alarm and survived. This crime was noted by many international papers. (*The Times*)

1978: The first radio episode of *The Hitchhiker's Guide to the Galaxy*, a science-fiction comedy series by Douglas Adams, was transmitted on BBC Radio 4 today. It became a multimedia phenomenon.

MARCH 8TH

1702: Anne Stuart, the last Stuart, ascended the throne today. She married Prince George of Denmark, her second cousin once removed. Despite seventeen pregnancies, none of her children survived.

———•◆•———

1934: London County Council was taken over by the Labour party today for the first time. The Labou party held council until the London County Council's abolition in 1965. (*Daily Mail*)

———•◆•———

1941: A bomb destroyed the North Lodge of Buckingham Palace and the same night the Café de Paris was hit when two bombs hurtled down the ventilation shaft, landing directly in front of Snake-hips Johnson and his band. His head was blown clean off his shoulders, and thirty-three members of staff, band members and revellers were killed. At least 100 were injured. (*Daily Mail*)

———•◆•———

1966: Today marked the escalation of the turf war between the Kray and Richardson gangs in south-east London. Richard Hart, one of the Kray associates, was shot dead in a brawl at Mr Smith's Club in Rushey Green, Catford, looked after by the Richardsons for the owners. (*Rough Justice*, R. Parker)

MARCH 9TH

1950: Timothy Evans, aged twenty-five, was hanged at Pentonville Prison for the murder of his wife Beryl at No. 10 Rillington Place, Notting Hill. A simple man, he had, under duress, admitted to killing her. He was granted a posthumous pardon in 1966 and, finally in 2003, the independent assessor for the Home Office, Lord Brennan, accepted that his conviction and execution was a miscarriage of justice. (*Daily Mail*)

1966: At 8.30 p.m. Ronnie Kray, East End gangster, flanked by two Glaswegian minders, walked into the Blind Beggar Public house on Whitechapel Road. Kray shot rival gangster George Cornell through the head with a 9mm Mauser Automatic pistol. Cornell had been a childhood friend of Kray's, but had become a member of the rival Richardson gang. It had also been mooted that he had called Kray a 'fat poof', and that this was why he was killed. This crime eventually led to the imprisonment of the Kray twins. (*Daily Mail*)

1967: The Beatles recorded several tracks for 'Getting Better', a song that would eventually appear on the 'Sergeant Pepper' album, at EMI Studios Abbey Road, NW8. (*The Beatles: The Authorised Biography*, Hunter Davies)

MARCH 10TH

1906: The Baker Street and Waterloo underground line, between Baker Street and Lambeth North, was officially opened on this day. The *Evening News* coined the name 'Bakerloo' which stuck within a few months. Rumour had it that it was built and funded by a few businessmen who wanted to get to and from Lord's cricket ground as quickly as possible. (*Evening News*)

1914: Velazquez's painting of Venus and Cupid, also known as the 'Rokeby Venus', was slashed seven times with an axe in a political protest by suffragette Mary Richardson in the National Gallery. (*Evening News*)

1743: John Broughton established a boxing amphitheatre near Hanway Street, Oxford Street. He announced his first programme in the *Daily Advertiser* on this day, in which he put eight champions on the stage and invited the audience to pair them. Broughton is generally considered to be the father of English pugilism.

MARCH 11TH

1708: The Scottish Militia Bill was passed by the House of Commons and House of Lords in the spring of this year, but was vetoed by Queen Anne on the advice of her ministers on this day for fear that the proposed militia created would be disloyal. This was the last time that a British monarch vetoed legislation.

———◆———

1712: In the early hours of the morning, an assault was made on a watchman in Essex Street off the Strand. Some attackers, Mohocks, were apprehended and identified: Edward Lord Hitchinbrooke was bailed for £1,500; Sir Mark Cole, Baronet, was bailed for £900, Thomas Fanshawe, Thomas Sydenham, and others, gentlemen, were bailed at £400 each; Hugh Jones, servitor to Sir Mark Cole, was bailed at £40. (City of London Records Office)

———◆———

1881: Count Miecislas Jaraczewski, an accomplished man about town, was found dead by his own hand, of Prussic acid, at his flat in Bennett Street, St James. A friend of the Prince of Wales, he had just hosted a midnight supper at the Turf Club. His debts forced his hand. (*The Times*)

MARCH 12TH

1702: There had been regular newspapers before the *Daily Courant*, one of which – the *Courant*, published first in 1621 – nearly shared its name. The paper was started by Edward Mallet; is first edition, published on this day, Wednesday, consisted of one sheet, divided into two columns, publicising itself as a source of factual news. The paper first saw the light of day in Fleet Street – Mallet gave his address as next door to the King's Arms Tavern by Fleet Bridge.

———◆———

1709: 'A negro man named Limerick, lately come from Barbadoes, aged 16 years, a handsome tall fellow, to be dispos'd of. Enquiries at Madam England's near the Sun Tavern in Shadwell.' (*Daily Courant*)

———◆———

1794: The third Royal Drury Lane Theatre, designed by Henry Holland, , was opened today.

———◆———

1969: Paul McCartney, aged twenty-seven, married Linda Eastman, aged twenty-eight, at Marylebone Register office today. Hundreds of people gathered outside to catch a glimpse of the couple as they arrived with Miss Eastman's six-year-old daughter, Heather, from a previous marriage. (*Daily Mail*)

March 13th

1741: An advertisement gave notice on this day, 'that there is to be seen from eight in the morning to nine at night, at the end of the great booth at Blackheath, a West of England woman 38 years of age alive, with two heads, one above the other; having no hands nor fingers, nor toes, yet can she dress and undress, knit, sew, read, sing'. (Reprinted in *Merrie England in the Olden Times,* G. Daniel)

———◆———

1872: A libel case was brought to a sudden close on this day at Southwark Magistrate's Court. The plaintiff, Lady Twiss, wife of the Advocate General Sir Travers Twiss, had left London and England, never to return. A lawyer, Mr Chaffers, had accused her of not being the daughter of a Polish nobleman, but a common French prostitute who had before been part of a house of ill-repute and with whom Sir Travers had consorted before marrying. The forlorn husband retired from active life to a house in Fulham. (*The Times*)

MARCH 14TH

1805: William Betty, the most successful child actor of the nineteenth century, played Hamlet, aged fourteen, on the London stage. Today the House of Commons was adjourned to enable members to watch his performance. (*Daily Advertiser*)

1885: The premiere of the comic opera *The Mikado*, by W.S. Gilbert and Arthur Sullivan, was held at the Savoy Theatre.

1963: An Antiguan, John Edgecumbe, had been charged with shooting at a model, Christine Keeler, at the home of Dr Stephen Ward in Wimpole Mews, Marylebone, with intent to kill. He pleaded not guilty at the Old Bailey on this day. Unfortunately Miss Keeler had completely disappeared. (*Daily Mail*)

2008: Queen Elizabeth II officially opened Terminal 5 at Heathrow, exclusively used by British Airways. It opened for passengers on 27 March with flight 26 from Hong Kong arriving at 4.50 a.m. The first passenger to enter Terminal 5 was Paul Walker. (*Daily Mail*)

MARCH 15TH

1752: London was hit by a very strong gale. Two ships berthed at Vauxhall were smashed onto the shore. Chimneys were torn away, roofs blown off and a window in Westminster Abbey was destroyed. (*London Advertiser*)

———◆———

1909: On this day H. Gordon Selfridge, an American retailer, opened his store Selfridge in the unfashionable West End of Oxford Street. He coined two mottoes: 'Only – shopping days until Christmas' and 'business as usual' – sayings used to this day. (*Daily Mail*)

———◆———

1932: The first musical programme to come from the new Broadcasting House at Langham Place was given by Henry Hall and his dance orchestra. (BBC)

———◆———

2011: The BBC comedy series, '2012', set in the fictional offices of the Olympic Games' organisers, started on 14 March with a storyline featuring problems with the clock in Trafalgar Square – reality hit when on this day the real-life clock in Trafalgar Square broke! (*Evening Standard*)

MARCH 16TH

1872: The first English FA Cup final took place at the Oval. The Wanderers beat the Royal Engineers 1–0. (*History of the FA Cup*, The Football Association; *A History of Fotball*, Michael Heatley)

1912: The last four-horse team pulling an ordinary garden-seat bus, operated by Thomas Tilling, ran today from the foot of Balham Hill to Gracechurch Street. (LT Museum)

1941: On this Wednesday night the north-east corner of Leicester Square was hit: a land mine fell into Jermyn Street; another struck the Newport buildings in Shaftesbury Avenue killing forty-eight and injuring eighty-three; Shaftesbury Theatre was destroyed; Christie's was burnt out; and Stone's Chop House in Panton Street was obliterated. (*Evening News*)

2009: Full construction of the London Bridge Tower, nicknamed 'the Shard', started today. Designed by the architect Renzo Piano, the Shard will be the tallest inhabited building in Europe for a short time, at 310m in height, with fifty floors excavated for the foundations. (*Evening Standard*)

MARCH 17TH

1845: In this year, Stephen Perry, of the rubber manufacturing company Messers Perry & Co., invented the rubber band to hold papers or envelopes together. On this day Perry patented the rubber band. These first rubber bands were made of vulcanised rubber. (Patent Office)

1921: Dr Marie Stopes and her second husband, Humphrey Roe, opened the Mother's Clinic at No. 61 Marlborough Road, Holloway. The clinic, run by midwives, offered mothers birth control, advice and taught them the use of a cervical cap. She edited the newsletter *Birth Control News*. Her sex manual *Married Love* was controversial and influential, whilst her book, *Wise Parenthood*, was written before she had become a parent. Never in favour of abortion, she argued that prevention of conception sufficed. (*Oxford Dictionary of National Biography*)

1968: A largely peaceful anti-Vietnam War rally of about 10,000 in Trafalgar Square turned violent when the protesters marched to the American Embassy in Grosvenor Square. Police in their hundreds surrounded the embassy and, when the protesters refused to back off, violence flared. There were ninety-one police casualties, and 246 protesters were arrested, seven of which were imprisoned. (*Daily Mail* – Hansard)

MARCH 18TH

1745: Robert Walpole died at his house in Arlington Street. He is considered Britain's first 'prime minister' as he was the first minister of a cabinet-style government responsible for parliament.

———•◆•———

1789: Catherine Murphy, a counterfeiter, was hanged outside Newgate Prison and then burned at the stake. She was the last person to be burned at the stake. The law was changed in 1790 for the benefit of the officers who were offended by the stench of the burning meat. (*Newgate Calendar*)

———•◆•———

1894: Croydon was on this Sunday night the scene of a curious transaction – a labouring man selling his wife for a pot of fourpenny ale. The purchaser adopted the precaution of taking a receipt for his money. (*Hereford Journal*)

———•◆•———

1932: The first news bulletin from Broadcasting House in Langham Place was read by Stuart Hibberd on this day. (BBC Archives)

———•◆•———

1949: From this day, shop windows were allowed to be lit up after closing time, and to use flashing advertisement signs. (*Evening News*)

MARCH 19TH

1721: An act was passed for the rebuilding of St-Martin-in the-Fields in 1720. The commissioners selected James Gibbs to design the new church. The foundation stone was laid today by King George I 'with full religious and Masonic rites', and the last stone of the spire was placed in position in December 1724. The total cost was £33,661, including the architect's fees. (*Survey of London, Vol.20*)

❖

1958: Madame Tussaud's opened the London Planetarium today on the site of an old cinema that was destroyed in the Second World War. It seated around 330 beneath a horizontal dome. An opto-mechanical star projector offered the audience a show based on a view of the night sky as seen from earth. It was the UK's first planetarium and ceased operation in 2006. (*The Times*)

❖

1986: On this day mounting speculation was brought to an abrupt end when a Buckingham Palace press officer walked to crowds of journalists outside the gates and handed out headed notepaper announcing the engagement of Prince Andrew and Sarah Ferguson. This is also Prince Andrew's birthday. (*The Times*)

MARCH 20TH

1712: John Deabins, a knight of the Middle Temple, was indicted for an assault on a merchant. He had had several accomplices but all had escaped. (Sessions file)

———◆◆———

1819: Lord George Cavendish acquired Burlington House and decided to create a commercial establishment alongside. Annoyed by the constant litter being dropped on his premises, he asked an architect to build him a roofed arcade – Burlington Arcade was opened on this day. (*Victoria County Histories*)

———◆◆———

1966: The football World Cup was stolen while on exhibition at Central Hall in Westminster, London. The £30,000 solid gold Jules Rimet trophy disappeared while a church service was taking place in another part of the building. Thieves removed the cup from the 'Sport with Stamps' display at the Stampex exhibition, but stamps worth £3m were left behind. It was, however, found by a mongrel dog while out for a walk in South London on 27 March. (*Daily Mail*)

———◆◆———

1974: Ian Ball fired six shots in an attempt to kidnap Princess Ann while she was being driven down Pall Mall. (*The Times*)

MARCH 21ST

1829: The Duke of Wellington and the Earl of Winchilsea duelled at Battersea Fields today. Winchilsea was irked by Wellington's support of the Catholics. Both took care not to hit the other. This date is celebrated by King's College as 'Duel Day' as Wellington helped establish King's as a university college.

———◆———

1922: Waterloo station was formally opened by Queen Mary. Work had started on rebuilding it in 1909, but the war had interrupted work. (*The Times*)

———◆———

1963: On this day the Home Secretary was asked to scotch the rumours circulating about Michael Profumo, a minister. They related to a Christine Keeler, a Mandy Davies and a shooting by a West Indian, as well as their relationship with Yevgeni Ivanov, a Russian attaché. Mr Profumo told the house that no impropriety whatsoever had occurred. On 5 June he admitted he had misled the House and would resign. (*Guardian*)

———◆———

1990: A massive Poll Tax demonstration in Trafalgar Square turned into a riot; 417 people were injured and 341 arrested. (*Daily Mail*)

MARCH 22ND

1774: *Tommy Thumb's Song Book, a collection of Nursery Rhymes for all little Masters and Misses; to be sung to them by their Nurses 'till they can sing themselves* by Nurse Lovechild was published by Mary Cooper and advertised by the *London Evening Post* on this day. This first known compilation of nursery rhymes included 'Baah Baah Black Sheep'.

1888: The Football League was founded at a meeting at Anderton's Hotel in Fleet Street, attended by representatives from twelve clubs. (FA)

1907: The first cabs with taxi-meters began operating in London, the fee being 8*d* per mile. (London Taxi Cab Association)

2000: Cardinal Cormac Murphy O'Connor was today installed as the tenth Archbishop of Westminster, head of the Roman Catholic Church in England. He resigned in 2009 and Vincent Nichols was appointed as his successor. As the first Archbishop of Westminster to resign, he is the first to become Archbishop Emeritus of Westminster. (*The Times*)

MARCH 23RD

1743: King George II attended the first London performance of Handel's *Messiah*. In the middle of the *Hallelujah Chorus* the King, so overcome with emotion, rose to his feet in appreciation. The entire audience followed suit out of respect for his majesty. So began the custom of standing during the singing of the *Hallelujah Chorus*. A James Beattie related this incident some thirty-seven years later …

1861: London's first trams began operating form Bayswater, designed by Mr Train of New York. (London Transport Museum)

1889: Instigated by Sir Joseph Bazalgette using powers granted in the Metropolitan Board of Works (Various Powers) Act 1885, the Woolwich Free Ferry officially opened on this day – two days before the Metropolitan Board of Works was replaced by the London County Council. (*Official Ferry History*)

1964: A coaching inn stood on the site of Jack Straw's Castle on West Heath Road, Hampstead, from 1721. A Second World War bomb wrecked it. It rose again from the ashes and was reopened on this day displaying a castellated and weather-boarded exterior. It is now flats. (*Hampstead and Highgate News*)

MARCH 24TH

1809: Drury Lane Theatre burnt to the ground while its owner Sheridan was waiting to speak in the House of Commons. When the news of the fire arrived, a move was made to adjourn the debate. He objected on the grounds that private calamity should not interfere with private business. He later bought a glass of wine while watching the fire, uttering, 'a man must surely be allowed to take a glass of wine by his own fire-side?' (*Morning Chronicle*)

———◆———

1918: Chung Ling Soo, the most famous 'Chinese' magician to grace the London stage, died on this day after a gun in his most famous trick fired a real bullet at him the night before. When shot he cried out, 'Oh my God, something's happened, bring down the curtain' – his first English words since the bigamist and American conman William Ellsworth Robinson adopted his Chinese persona – his best trick yet. (*Daily Mail*)

———◆———

2007: This Saturday was witness to almost 4,000 people walking the 'Walk of Witness', from Whitehall and Clapham, the home of the Clapham Saints, converging on Kennington to mark the bicentenary of the Act of the Abolition of the Slave Trade. (*Daily Mail*)

MARCH 25TH

1748: A fire broke out in a Peruke Maker's house in Exchange Alley early this morning. Despite the best efforts, the blaze continued. By noon three people had died and over 100 houses were destroyed, one of which was the birthplace of Thomas Gray. (British Library)

———◆———

1843: The Thames Tunnel from Rotherhithe to Wapping was opened on this day. It was the first underwater tunnel and the only joint venture between Marc and Isambard Brunel. It was started in 1825 and it is a tribute to the Brunels that refurbishment was only needed for the first time in the 1990s. (London Transport Museum)

———◆———

1975: Four hundred members of the National Front, beating drums and chanting 'We're going to get the Reds', marched through Islington waving placards. They were protesting against integration with Europe. (*Guardian*)

———◆———

2010: Simmering tensions between students of two West London schools led to a twenty-strong gang hunting down and stabbing to death Sofyen Belamouadden, aged fifteen, in front of horrified commuters at Victoria station. (*Daily Mail*)

MARCH 26TH

1780: Mrs E. Johnson's *British Gazette and Sunday Monitor*, the first Sunday newspaper, was published today. It ceased publication in 1829.

———◆———

1791: His Majesty's Theatre in the Haymarket, built on the site of its burnt-out predecessor, was opened on this day. It was the largest in England and, because of the monopoly on plays enjoyed by all the other theatres, it presented only operas. (*Annual Register*)

———◆———

1862: George Peabody, an American banker settled in London, announced the creation of a fund to ameliorate the condition of the poor and needy in London. He added that this munificence was in partial repayment for the 'courtesy, kindness and confidence' he had received from the British people. (*The Times*)

———◆———

1973: Ten newly elected lady members of the Stock Exchange were admitted on this day for the first time. The next hurdle will be to allow women dealers onto the floor. (*Guardian*)

MARCH 27TH

1793: Wednesday – a note appeared outside the 'Royal Bun House, Chelsea, Good Friday. No Cross Buns. Mrs Hand respectfully informs her friends and the public, that in consequence of the great concourse of people which assembled before her house at a very early hour, on the morning of Good Friday last, by which her neighbours ... have been much alarmed ...; it having also been intimated, that to encourage or countenance a tumultuous assembly at this particular period might be attended with consequences more serious than have hitherto been apprehended; desirous, therefore, of testifying her regard and obedience to those laws by which she is happily protected, she is determined, though much to her loss, not to sell Cross Buns on that day to any person whatever, but Chelsea buns as usual.'

———◆———

1953: On this day the bodies of four women were found at No. 10 Rillington Place, Notting Hill, by the police. John Christie, a tenant, couldn't be sure how many women he had murdered. He never did admit responsibility for the deaths of the wife and daughter of another tenant, Timothy Evans. Timothy Evans was hanged for their deaths previously and was eventually posthumously pardoned. (*Guardian*)

MARCH 28TH

1727: Sir Isaac Newton, the scientist, was buried in Westminster Abbey on this day; his body had lain in state in the Jerusalem Chamber beforehand. His funeral was attended by Voltaire, who was astonished to note that some of the greatest peers of the realm attended – something that would never happen in France! (*Lettres d'Angleterre*, C. de Saussure)

———•◆•———

1925: Cambridge University won the boat race this year, as Oxford sank. Oxford sank again in 1951. Cambridge's boat first sank in 1859. The only time Cambridge's boat sank again was in 1978.

———•◆•———

1979: Margaret Thatcher, leader of the Conservatives, brought a vote of no confidence in the Labour government led by James Callaghan. This was an important step towards her becoming the first female Prime Minister of the UK. (*Guardian*)

MARCH 29TH

1871: Queen Victoria officially opened the Central Hall of Arts and Sciences. She renamed it the Prince Albert Hall of Arts and Sciences as a tribute to her dead husband. (*The Times*)

———◆◆———

1920: Croydon Airport opened today. It owed its existence to two world war airfields, Beddington and Waddon Aerodromes, on each side of Plough Lane. The decision was taken to combine the two airfields to make them the 'Airport of London'. The two halves were linked by a level crossing, where cars had to be halted at first by a man with a red flag, and later by a gate. (*Wallington & Carshalton Times*)

———◆◆———

1981: The first London Marathon was run on this day. It was founded by former Olympic champion Chris Brasher and Welsh athlete John Disley. The race began at Blackheath and finished at the Mall alongside St James's Park. It originally had about 6,700 runners and now has over 36,00; it is now the largest fundraising event in the world. (*The Times*)

MARCH 30TH

1855: The Compagnie Generale des Omnibus de Londres was incorporated today and soon became the largest omnibus operator in London. Within a year it controlled 600 operators in London, a taste of the present bus system – a large proportion of which is owned by RATP, a French company. (*The Times*)

1912: On this Saturday Oxford and Cambridge bravely battled once more in the Thames Boat Race against high winds that sank the Cambridge crew and nearly sank the Oxford crew. Oxford managed to empty their boat and limp in to the finish despite F.E. Pitman, the umpire, declaring it a no race. It was rescheduled for Monday 1 April when Oxford won by six lengths. (*The Times*)

1979: Shadow Northern Ireland Secretary Airey Neave was killed by a car bomb outside the House of Commons. (*Daily Mail*)

1984: Peter Yarrall, 59 stone, Britain's heaviest man who suffered from a glandular disorder, died at his flat in East Ham today. A crane and ten firemen had to be used to get his corpse out of his flat. (*Evening Standard*)

MARCH 31ST

1668: The 'Ring' or 'Tour' was an inner circle in the centre of the northern half of Hyde Park, where it was fashionable to ride and drive. Pepys recorded today that he 'took up my wife and Deb to the Park, where being in a hackney, and they undressed, was ashamed to go into the Tour, but went round the Park, and so with pleasure home'.

1869: Deptford Dockyard, founded in 1513, was finally closed today. It was bought by Mr T.P. Austin for £70, 000. He sold part of it to the Corporation of London for £94, 640, for a market for foreign cattle, opened in 1871.

1924: The first British national airline, Imperial Airways, was founded at Croydon Airport. (*Croydon Post*)

1986: Lady Gale, the tenant of the apartment in the south wing of Hampton Court Palace, died in a fire that caused several million pounds' worth of damage to the building. (*Evening Standard*)

1986: On this day the Greater London Council ceased to exist. London was without an overall administration for the first time since 1855. (*The Times*)

April 1st

1819: *The Times* reported that an unfortunate accident happened on the previous Tuesday. Mr Bellasis, son of the late Dr Bellasis, was crossing the New Road near the Small Pox Hospital, he was knocked down by the pole of a carriage which was passing, and before the coachman had time to draw up his horses the fore wheel of the carriage had passed over his neck – the vital spark was extinct.

———•◆•———

1841: Kew Gardens today became a public facility. The initial 9 acres would shortly be enlarged to 46. (*The Times*)

———•◆•———

1875: Richard Horatio Edgar Freeman was born at No. 7 Ashburnham Grove, Greenwich, to Mary Jane Richards, an actress. His biological father, Richard Edgar, never knew of his existence. He was to become one of the most prolific authors of all time and the originator of *King Kong*, as Edgar Wallace. (*Oxford Dictionary of National Biography*)

———•◆•———

2010: The *Daily Mail* reported that Tower Bridge had just been sold to an American, Daniel Horwendil, for £133 million. It would be used as a centrepiece of an 'English theme park'. The bid was deemed too high a figure to be refused.

April 2nd

1914: The Geffrye Museum of Furniture was opened in Kingsland Road in a set of fourteen almshouses and a chapel erected by the Ironmongers Co. in 1715. The nearby Shoreditch area was the centre of furniture manufacture. (*The Times*)

———•◆•———

1928: Charles Lindbergh landed at Croydon Airport today. The local press commented that, 'one gets the immediate impression that civil aviation in England has been established …' It was the first major civil airport in the world.

———•◆•———

1962: The first 'Panda' crossing was inaugurated in York Road opposite Waterloo station by Ernest Marples, the Minister of Transport. The black and white triangular marking with a sequence of flashing lights caused confusion with both pedestrians and motorists; the scheme was eventually abandoned. (*Daily Mail*)

———•◆•———

2009: The leaders of the world's twenty leading economies, the G20, met today at the Excel Centre in East London, to plan action on the spread of the world financial crisis. (*The Times*)

APRIL 3RD

1712: Capt. Thomas Seaman and Mr Edward Churchill, gentlemen, assaulted 'without provocation' Robert Cutmore, a servant, off St James's Square. Both were indicted for 'assault and on suspicion of being Mohocks'. They were held for two days and bailed for £400 on 5 April. (Court of Sessions)

1913: On this day Emmeline Pankhurst was sentenced to three years in prison for inciting supporters to place explosives at the London home of Chancellor of the Exchequer David Lloyd George on 19 February. (*The Times*)

1933: The first automatic traffic lights in London were installed on this day in Trafalgar Square. (*Pathé*, Police Archives)

1954: The 100th Oxford and Cambridge Boat Race at Putney was won by Oxford in rough conditions. (*The Times*)

1965: The Elephant and Castle Shopping Centre, a bleak modernist architectural edifice of 120 units and a tower, was opened today by Ray Gunter, Minister of Labour. Only thirty-five units were taken prior to completion. The whole scheme is presently under review. (*The Times*)

APRIL 4TH

1942: Gordon Cumming, an air cadet, dubbed the Blackout Ripper, was tried on this day for the murder of Evelyn Oatley, a prostitute. He was hanged during an air raid on 25 June at Wandsworth Prison. A gas mask with his name on it, carelessly dropped at an attempted attack on a young woman, led to his arrest. He had killed at least three women. (*Daily Express*)

———◆———

1581: On this day a great ceremony took place in Deptford Creek, the knighting of Admiral Drake aboard the *Golden Hind*. Many thousands attended, and a makeshift walkway erected for spectators collapsed halfway through the ceremony, spilling many spectators into the creek to the amusement of the crowd. He was knighted by a French nobleman, the Marquis de Marchaumont, the French ambassador, not the Queen. This was to avoid drawing attention to Drake's achievements and making it seem that she disapproved of his tactics, to appease the Spanish.

———◆———

1981: Oxford University's first woman cox, twenty-three-year-old Susan Brown, steered her crew to victory over Cambridge University in the annual Boat Race. (*Evening Standard*)

April 5th

1742: The Ranelagh Gardens pleasure gardens in the grounds of Ranelagh House, were opened on this day with a breakfast. They were eventually closed and the house was pulled down in 1804.

<hr>

1955: On this day Queen Elizabeth II officially accepted Winston Churchill's resignation as Prime Minister. He was eighty-one. (*The Times*)

<hr>

1968: Flt-Lt Alan Pollock, unimpressed that the RAF was not going to celebrate its fiftieth anniversary, decided, without authorisation, to fly a Hawker Hunter towards Tower Bridge. On landing he was arrested and discharged from the RAF. (*Evening Standard*)

<hr>

1973: The Department of Health & Social Security declared London 'a smallpox infected area' when three cases of the disease were confirmed. By 9 April health officials confirmed that the epidemic was now under control. The initial outbreak was at a London hospital and one of the sufferers died on 6 April. (*The Times*)

April 6th

1580: An earthquake struck London on this day at about 6 p.m., just as the Pope was trying to dislodge Elizabeth as Queen. Half a dozen chimney stacks and a pinnacle at Westminster Abbey came down. There was only one reported fatality, Thomas Grey, an apprentice cobbler, killed by falling masonry. This was the largest recorded earthquake in England. (*Churchyard letters*)

———◆———

1955: Sir Anthony Eden, Secretary of State for Foreign Affairs, became Prime Minister today in succession to Sir Winston Churchill.

———◆———

1973: An early Plantagenet fountain found under New Palace Yard, Westminster, was removed on this day during the rebuilding of the new car park for MPs, and would eventually be relocated once the car park was finished and the upper ground grassed, Mr Channon told *The Times* on this day.

———◆———

2007: An estimated 4,000 silent dancers converged at Victoria station in a 'flash mob' at 6.53 p.m. They danced, Ipods to their ears, for two hours, until the police dispersed them. (*Evening Standard*)

APRIL 7TH

1779: On this day actress, singer and mistress of the Earl of Sandwich, Martha Ray, was murdered by a jealous spurned admirer. James Hackman, a clergyman, shot her on this Wednesday evening outside the Covent Garden Theatre where she had been watching Isaac Bickerstaffe's comic opera *Love in a Village*. He tried to commit suicide, but failed, and was tried and hanged a few days later. (*Watford Observer*)

1903: George Chapman, also known as Severin Klosowski, a Polish barber and publican, was hanged today at Wandsworth Prison for the murder of Maud Marsh, his wife, with poison. He had married three other English women who had all died under suspicious circumstances. Many, including Inspector John Abberline, the policeman in charge of the Ripper cases, thought that Chapman was Jack the Ripper.

1908: Herbert Henry Asquith of the Liberal party took office as Prime Minister today. He served from 1908-1916 and was the longest continuing serving Prime Minister until 1988. He was forced to travel to Biarritz for the official 'kissing of the hands' of the monarch. This was the only time a British Prime Minister has formally taken office on foreign soil. (*Oxford Dictionary of National Biography*)

April 8th

1663: The first playbill was issued from Drury Lane: 'By his majestie, his company of comedians at the New Theatre in Drury Lane will be acted a comedy called *The Humorous Lieutenant*'.

———◆———

1694: Philadelphia Pyke, wife of Benjamin, was charged before the Lord Mayor with being a disorderly lewd woman and 'to have seduced and drawn aside Thomas Prichett, ye apprentice of john Garrett in Ivy Lane, scrivener'. (City of London Records Office)

———◆———

1953: A central line train to Epping crashed into a stationary train in a tunnel at Leyton. The second coach of the Epping train telescoped into the tunnel, killing eleven people. (*East Ham Recorder*)

———◆———

1989: The longest single movement work in Western musical history, the symphony *Odyssey* by Nicholas Maw, received its first complete performance in London, in the BBC Proms – 'ninety-six minutes punctuated by resonating time-chords inspired by the composer's grandfather clock'. (*The Times*)

APRIL 9TH

1626: Francis Bacon, philosopher, scientist and statesman, died of pneumonia on this day. He had experimented trying to freeze a chicken with snow, but caught a chill and was taken to the Earl of Arundel's house in Highgate to recuperate. However, the bed was damp and he never rose from it. (*Who's Who in Stuart Britain*, C.P. Hill)

1747: Simon Fraser, 11th Lord Lovat, an octogenarian and one of the three Scottish peers caught in the Jacobite Rebellion, was beheaded on Tower Hill on this day. He was the last man to be executed on Tower Hill. A stand erected for spectators collapsed, killing twenty of them. (City of London Records Office)

1787: A fencing match between the mixed race Chevalier de St Georges and the *Chevalière* d'Eon took place today at Carlton House before the Prince of Wales. Both antagonists were considered fencers of the first class, but d'Eon, dressed as a woman and twenty years older than St Georges, won the bout. (*Angelo's Memoirs*)

1838: The present building housing the National Gallery was opened. (*The Times*)

APRIL 10TH

1633: The herbalist Thomas Johnson put a bunch of bananas in his shop window in Snow Hill. This was the first time that this fruit had been displayed for sale in England. (*Chambers' Book of Days*)

———◆———

1848: On this Monday, over 20,000 Chartists, not the millions expected, met at a rally at Kennington common, but by 2 p.m. there were no more than 100 people on the common – they had all dispersed. (*Illustrated London News*)

———◆———

1858: The Great Bell of Westminster, Big Ben, was cast in the Whitechapel foundry on this day. (*The Times*)

———◆———

1981: The Brixton Riot started. It lasted two days. Tensions had been fuelled by unemployment and lack of social housing. These boiled over when a black youth was stabbed, was taken to hospital by the police and reputedly left to die. The riot resulted in 280 injuries to police, forty-five to the public, more than 100 vehicles burned and 150 buildings damaged. (*The Times*)

APRIL 11TH

1554: Sir Thomas Wyatt, leader of a rebellion against Mary Tudor, was beheaded on Tower Hill having been tried for high treason on 15 March.

———◆·———

1653: On this day John Evelyn states in his diary that he 'went to take aire in Hyde Park, when every coach was made to pay a shilling and horse sixpence, by the sordid fellow who had purchased it of the State'.

———◆·———

1689: William III and Mary II were crowned joint monarchs of Great Britain by the Bishop of London Henry Compton. The Archbishop of Canterbury refused to officiate. (*London Gazette*)

———◆·———

1864: A London correspondent of the *Siècle* newspaper wrote on Giuseppe Garibaldi's arrival in London, '... I did not know what ardent sympathy there is in these devoted hearts, or what treasures of administration for liberty are hidden under that calm and almost cold exterior of the English. The reception of Garibaldi by the people of London is a fact without parallel'.

———◆·———

1914: The first British performance of George Bernard Shaw's *Pygmalion* took place today at His Majesty's Theatre, Haymarket with Mrs Patrick Campbell in the lead. (*The Times*)

APRIL 12TH

1709: Today was the publication of the first edition of an innovative journal, *The Tatler*. It appeared two or three times a week for the next two years and relied on parodies of celebrities by its editor Isaac Bickerstaff Esq., otherwise known as Richard Steele. (*The Tatler*)

———◆———

1953: Lionel Loague, an Australian actor and speech therapist, died at his residence Princes Court, Brompton Road today. He is reputed to have helped King George VI with his stammer. (*London Gazette*)

———◆———

1989: Andrew Lloyd Webber's musical *Cats* was performed today for the 3,358th time at the New London Theatre, Drury Lane. Premiered on 11 May 1981, this became London's longest running musical. It finished its run in 2002. *Les Miserables* has since then become London's longest running musical.

April 13th

1459: On this day there was a pitched battle between the men of the Fleete Streete area and men from the Court of Westminster. (Stow)

———◆———

1576: James Burbage, the actor manager, leased a piece of land on which he built London's first playhouse. At the end of the theatre's twenty-one-year lease, it was dismantled and reassembled on Bankside as 'the Globe'. (Curtain Road)

———◆———

1668: On this day John Dryden, literary critic, translator and poet, was appointed Poet Laureate. He was later appointed Royal Historiographer in 1670. He refused to take the oath of allegiance on William's accession and had previously converted to Catholicism, and was consequently dismissed. His is credited with bringing the word 'biography' into the English language. (*Oxford Dictionary of National Biography*)

———◆———

1740: On this day a former workshop at the Woolwich Warren became the Military Academy by Royal Warrant of King George II. Here the 100 fee-paying students studied Maths, Engineering, the Art of Fortification and Artillery.

APRIL 14TH

1471: The Battle of Barnet, just outside Barnet, was a decisive engagement in the Wars of the Roses fought on this day. Edward IV led the House of York whilst Henry VI led the House of Lancaster. This and the subsequent Battle of Tewkesbury marked the downfall of the House of Lancaster and the rise of the House of York.

———•◆•———

1857: Princess Beatrice, the fifth daughter and youngest of the nine children of Queen Victoria, was born on this day at Buckingham Palace. This birth caused controversy as it was announced that the Queen would use chloroform administered by Dr John Snow to seek relief from the pains of delivery. Both the Church of England and the medical establishment considered this dangerous to mother and child. (*The Times*)

———•◆•———

1913: On this Monday the Royal Geographical Society moved to new premises at Kensington Gore. The area is called 'Hot and Cold Corner' after the adjacent statues of David Livingstone and Sir Ernest Shackleton, famous for the Tropics and Antarctica respectively. (*Journal of the Royal Geographical Society*)

APRIL 15TH

1644: Sir Matthew Brand, owner of the most famous London theatre, the Globe, ordered it to be demolished. (*Guildhall Library*)

———◆·———

1936: The Swastika-draped coffin of the German ambassador, Leopold von Hoesch, a liberal, was accorded a ceremonial cortège through London and a nineteen-gun salute. Thousands of Londoners lined the route in silence, some making the Nazi salute, to Victoria station. His replacement was Joachim von Ribbentrop. (*The Times*)

———◆·———

1984: This evening the comedian Tommy Cooper collapsed from a heart attack in front of millions of television viewers, midway through his act on the LWT weekend variety show live from Her Majesty's Theatre. His collapse was considered part of the act and he was pronounced dead on arrival at hospital. (*Daily Mail*)

———◆·———

2008: *The Times* reported that William Lyttle, a retired engineer nicknamed the 'Mole-Man', spent forty years excavating a maze of tunnels beneath his Victorian property in Hackney and was facing a bill of almost £300,000 from the London borough of Hackney to cover the cost of repairs after his house nearly collapsed.

APRIL 16TH

1818: Abraham Norton was acquitted today of raping and murdering Mary Ashford. He had claimed his right by combat with his accuser, which was allowed by the court. His accuser, however, refused to fight. (*Gentleman's Magazine*)

1885: Mrs Mary Jeffries, owner of three brothels in Kensington, a flagellation house in Hampstead and a Chamber of Horrors in Gray's Inn Road, was today charged with keeping a disorderly house at the Middlesex Sessions. She arrived at Court on 5 May in a brougham, pleaded guilty, was fined £200 and bailed for £200. She paid one and a titled officer stood surety for the other. She was back in business the next day. (*Pall Mall Gazette*)

1892: 'Pedestrian, London, W' wrote a letter to *The Times* today complaining that 'the growing number of cyclists is resulting in a Tyranny of the Road' and that his country walks were 'regularly interrupted by hurtling wheelmen like a horde of Apache or Sioux Indians ... woe betide the luckless man or aught else coming their way ... can nothing be done?' (*The Times*)

APRIL 17TH

1941: Albert Alex Bowlly, better known as Albert Allick or Al Bowlly, singer, songwriter, composer and bandleader, was killed by a parachute mine that exploded outside his flat in Duke Street, W1. He was buried in a mass grave at the Westminster Cemetery, Hanwell. (Pathé)

1965: On this day Paul McCartney spent the day shopping for furniture in Portobello Road, disguised in a cloth cap, moustache, glasses and overcoat. (*Rock History*, Mitch Michaels)

1984: On this Tuesday at 10.18 a.m., during an anti-Gadaffi rally at the Libyan People's Bureau, No. 5 St James's Square, W1, shots were fired from a window at the Bureau, one of which killed PC Yvonne Fletcher, a few yards away from her fiancé who was also a policeman. (*Evening Standard*)

1999: A nail bomb exploded in Brixton, injuring at least forty-five people. Four of the casualties were seriously hurt and kept in hospital overnight. A market trader was handed a bag containing a nail bomb but it exploded before the police could disarm it. It was thought that the target was the largely black clientele of Brixton Market. (*Daily Mail*)

APRIL 18TH

1839: The Chelsea Bun House, a one-storey building with a colonnade projecting over the Pimlico Road pavement, noted for its delicious buns, was sold on this day. It was subsequently pulled down. (*The Times*)

———◆———

1931: The Dorchester Hotel, designed by Sir Owen Williams and William Curtis Green and built by Sir Robert McAlpine, opened onthis day. It became the headquarters of General Eisenhower during the Second World War. (*The Times*)

———◆———

1960: An estimated 60-100,000 people attended a 'Ban the Bomb' rally organised by the Campaign for Nuclear Disarmament in Trafalgar Square. (*Daily Mail*)

———◆———

1968: John Rennie's 1825 London Bridge was sold to Robert P. McCulloch of McCulloch Oil for $2,460,000 – it was subsequently disassembled, the pieces numbered and reassembled at Lake Havasu City. (*Evening News*)

———◆———

1988: The sixteenth-century symbol of the Speaker's authority, the Mace, was damaged by Ron Brown, a Labour MP, when he flung it to the floor during a debate on the Poll Tax. (*Guardian*)

APRIL 19TH

1012: Captured in his bishopric by marauding Danes, the Saxon Alphege, Archbishop of Canterbury, was held in Greenwich. The Danes lost patience over the lack of any ransom (Alphege had specifically requested that none be paid) and on this day supposedly threw ox bones at him and axe-butted him to death. The present church of St Alphege stands where he was martyred. (*A Brief History of the Anglo Saxons*, Hindley)

1710: Four Indian chiefs of the Mohawk and Algonquin tribes were received as diplomats by Queen Anne in London today. They requested military aid against the French, and Anglican missionaries to offset the French Jesuit conversions. (Dean R. Snow)

1951: The first Miss World Beauty Contest was held today in London. Devised by Eric Morley, an executive with Mecca Ltd, it coincided with the Festival of Britain. Of the thirty contestants only five were foreign – Kiki Haakonson, a Stockholm policeman's daughter, won. (*The Times*)

APRIL 20TH

1768: Hard economic times hit the poor first. Industrial conflict heightened, especially when John Wilkes returned to England. Coalheavers were one of the more powerful groups who demanded better wages. On this night they attacked the Roundabout Tavern owned by one John Green – he had advertised for people willing to work at his prices. They shouted 'Wilkes and Liberty'. He held out until the morning, escaped and was placed in Newgate for his safety. (*Newgate Calendar*)

1901: The final tie for the FA Cup was between Tottenham Hotspur and Sheffield United at Crystal Palace, Sydenham; 114,000 people attended and it ended with a 2-2 draw. It would be replayed at Bolton a week later. (*Illustrated London News*)

1955: On this Wednesday Thomas Bolitho, aged sixty-four, of St Martin's Lane, was sentenced to twenty-one months' imprisonment for stealing the first Strasbourg edition of *La Marseillaise* from the British Museum. Mr Bolitho stated that he had taken it to call attention to an injustice. (*The Times*)

APRIL 21ST

1834: On this Monday a meeting was held on Copenhagen Fields, Islington, to protest at the savagery of the sentence inflicted on the Tolpuddle Martyrs – the six had been transported to Australia for creating a Trade Union. About 30,000 marched to Downing Street from Islington after the meeting. (*The Times*)

1894: George Bernard Shaw's *Arms and the Man* premiered in London at the Royal Avenue Theatre, Northumberland Avenue, off Trafalgar Square (now the Playhouse Theatre). It was one of his first commercial successes. (*The Times*)

1955: On this day 700 printing machinery maintenance men for the newspaper industry stopped their strike at Fleet Street after nearly a month. (*Evening News*)

1955: On this Thursday the BBC announced that the Conservative and Labour parties would each have four election broadcasts on radio and three on television. The Liberal party would have one of each.

APRIL 22ND

1884: An earthquake centred in Essex was felt by workmen working at the top of Victoria Tower. It reportedly swayed 4in. (*The Times*)

———◆•———

1760: The first recorded use of roller skates was in 1743, but the details are lost to history. On this day, however, Jean-Joseph Merlin of Huy in the province of Liège, an instrument maker and inventor, attended a masquerade in central London on a pair of roller skates, playing a violin, to publicise his invention. Unfortunately he had not mastered how to stop and, trying to avoid the crowds, crashed into a large wall mirror. (John H. Lienhard)

———◆•———

1993: At 10.30 p.m. the eighteen-year-old black A-level student Stephen Lawrence was stabbed to death by a group of white men on the corner of Well Hall Road and Dickson Road, Eltham. Five suspects were arrested but not convicted. (*Daily Mail*)

APRIL 23RD

1390: A joust was held between Lord Welles, Ambassador to Scotland, and Sir David de Lindsay, a Scot, on London Bridge. This was a result of an argument as to the valour of the two nations – on the third run Welles was unseated and Lindsay went to his aid. (City of London Records Office)

1898: On this Saturday the maiden journey of the first motorised double-decker bus , with a top speed of 12mph, ran from Gravesend to the City of London – 'every man, every woman and child in Long Acre and along Piccadilly stopped and stared at the vehicle as it thundered past ...'. (*The Times*)

1924: The British Empire Exhibition opened this Wednesday in miserable weather. Fifty-six countries of the empire took part and Sir Edward Elgar conducted a 3,000-strong choir to open it. (*The Times*)

1928: Sir Leo George Chiozza Money, a political economist and MP, and Miss Irene Savidge were both arrested this Monday and charged with indecent behaviour. They had been seen kissing in Hyde Park by a policeman – the case was dismissed. (*The Times*)

APRIL 24TH

1678: On this day the first recorded execution on Kennington Common took place; 'the day of execution Sarah Elston all dressed in white, with a vast multitude of people attending her. And after very solemn prayers offered on the said occasion, the fire was kindled, and giving two or three lamentable shrieks, she was deprived of both voice and life, and so burnt to ashes.' She was burnt alive for murdering her husband.

———•———

1963: HRH Princess Alexandra of Kent, daughter of Prince George Duke of Kent and Marina of Greece, married the Hon. Angus Ogilvy at Westminster Abbey. The marriage was attended by all the Royal Family and televised worldwide – an estimated 200 million people watched the broadcast. (*The Times*)

———•———

1993: At about 10 a.m. an IRA truck bomb exploded 7m from the church of St Ethelburg-the-Virgin within Bishopsgate, totally destroying it. First recorded in 1250, and suffering only modest damage in the Blitz, the church was rebuilt. (*Daily Telegraph*)

APRIL 25TH

1660: The Convention Parliament on this day voted for the restoration of King Charles II (it was the sixty-third anniversary of the birth of Oliver Cromwell). (Guildhall Library)

1682: A severe storm on this day flooded St James' Park and inundated river neighbourhoods. The Brentford Vestry noted in its minutes that a skiff could be rowed up its main street.

1719: Daniel Defoe's book *Robinson Crusoe* was first published today in London. By the end of the century it had had four editions. It was the first book written independent of mythology, history, legends or previous literature. It spawned similar stories and was published in every known language of the times. (*Oxford Dictionary of National Biography*)

1854: On this day Euphemia Gray left John Ruskin two envelopes at his house in Herne Hill – one with a wedding ring and another with a demand for divorce, after six years of unconsummated marriage. Some believed that her unfortunately timed period on their wedding night was the cause; others cited what could be termed 'body hair trauma', as Mr Ruskin was accustomed to hairless nudes in paintings. (*Oxford Dictionary of National Biography*)

April 26th

1871: On this Wednesday night the pregnant Jane Maria Clouson was found dying of a blow to the head in Kidbrooke Lane, Eltham, by a policeman. The police discovered that she was pregnant by her employer's son. A nearby bloodied hammer, seemingly purchased by young Mr Pook a few days previously, led them to arrest him. Despite reasonable evidence young Mr Pook was acquitted, helped by the strident voice of the press, his father's employers. It was not a popular verdict. (*The Times*)

1921: On this day the first motorcycle police patrols went on duty in London. (Police Archives)

1928: On this day the Duke of York, the future King George VI, and Lady Elizabeth Bowes-Lyons, were married at Westminster Abbey. (*The Times*)

1999: The popular TV presenter Jill Dando was murdered this Monday morning outside her home in Fulham. The single bullet fired had the mark of a professional hit. A local loner, nevertheless, Barry George, was convicted on flimsy evidence and later released. The case is still unresolved. (*Daily Mail*)

APRIL 27TH

1831: Apsley House, the London home of the Duke of Wellington, was targeted by 'an unruly and indecent mob' incensed by his opposition to the Reform Bill. They 'broke the windows ... and he caused to be put up those blinds which remain to this day as a record of the people's ingratitude'. (*Mr Raikes' Journal*)

1872: A correspondent of the *Pall Mall Gazette* vouches for this story: from 4 p.m. until 11:30 p.m. on Thursday, Nos 56 and 58 Reverdy Road, Bermondsey were assailed with stones and other missiles ... policemen could not trace from whence they were thrown.

1928: The Piccadilly Theatre designed by Bertie Crewe opened today. It was almost immediately taken over for films, but reverted to drama at the end of 1929. (*Variety*)

1970: The actor Tony Curtis was caught in possession of cannabis at Heathrow Airport and fined £50. He had flown in to star alongside Roger Moore in the long-running series 'The Persuaders'. (*The Times*)

April 28th

1772: The world's most travelled goat died today in London. She had circumnavigated the world twice, once with Capt. Wallis in the *Dolphin*, then on Cook's *Endeavour*. The Admiralty had signed a document vouching for her travels and longevity. (Minutes of the Royal Society)

1773: On this day White's club was destroyed by fire. A contemporary account noted that the fire began at night and that the owner's wife leapt 'out of window a pair stairs upon a feather-bed without much hurt'.

1870: Ernest Boulton and Frederick Park, Ernest wearing a cherry-coloured silk gown and Freddy wearing a dark-green satin dress, were arrested at the Strand Theatre and charged with 'conspiring and inciting persons to commit an unnatural offence'. 'Stella' and 'Fanny' respectively were subjected to a minute examination to establish if they had had anal sex. Their trial provided amusement and shock – but as the prosecution could not find any impropriety, they were found not guilty. (*The Times*)

1994: The Trustees of the Tate Gallery announced on this day that they were to take possession of the Bankside Power Station and convert it into a museum of Modern Art. (*The Times*)

APRIL 29TH

1376: Today the Speaker of the House of Commons, Sir Peter de La Mare, took office.

1826: On this Saturday a public meeting was held at the Horticultural Society chaired by Sir Stamford Raffles. He recommended the formation of a society, the object of which would be to import new breeds of animals from foreign parts. 'The Regent's Park is to be the headquarters … though we do not know how the inhabitants of the Park will like lions, leopards and lynxes so near their neighbourhood'. (*Literary Gazette*)

1947: On this Tuesday afternoon Jays' Jewellers in Charlotte Street was held up by three scarved and armed men. An alarm was turned on as the shopkeepers threw a stool at their assailants. The robbers panicked, and ran off shooting wildly. Finding their getaway car blocked, they ran into Alex de Antiquis on his motorbike and shot him dead. (*Daily Mail*)

1968: The Metropolitan Police force's first black woman, Fay Allen, aged twenty-nine, started work on this day in Croydon. (*Guardian*)

April 30th

1907: The Fifth Congress of the Russian Social Democratic Workers Party was held at the Brotherhood church on the corner of Southgate Road and Balmes Road, N1. It included Stalin, Lenin, Trotsky, Rosa Luxembourg and Maxim Gorky, and lasted until 19 May. (*Reminiscences of Lenin*)

1980: Gunmen took over the Iranian embassy at No. 27 Prince's Gate, demanding autonomy for Khuzestan and the release of political prisoners in Iran. Under the scrutiny of the media, the SAS stormed the building on 5 May, killing five people and releasing the hostages. (*Evening Standard*)

1999: On this Bank Holiday Friday evening, the Admiral Duncan pub in Old Compton Street was torn apart by a nail bomb placed inside. Three people were killed and seventy-nine injured. The perpetrator, a committed National Socialist, was identified from CCTV and imprisoned. (*Daily Mail*)

MAY 1ST

1416: The Holy Roman Emperor, Sigismund, arrived in London today in an attempt to mediate between Henry V and the French. He was installed at the Palace of Westminster. (Guildhall Library)

———◆———

1421: London's first public lavatory, paid for by Richard Whittington, was most probably erected this day. 'Whittington's Longhouse', as it was known, contained two long rows each of sixty-four seats, one side for men, and the other for women. (Guildhall Library)

———◆———

1517: A mob, upwards of 1,000 young, angry apprentices and labourers, rampaged through the City destroying property and assaulting anyone in their path. They were angry that foreigners, namely French, were being employed rather than the native population. (City of London Records Office)

———◆———

1912: A statue of Peter Pan blowing his pipe on a stump of a tree, with fairies and mice and squirrels all around, appeared as if by magic on this morning in Kensington Gardens. Sir James Barrie had commissioned the work in secret and had it erected in the wee small hours. (*The Times*)

MAY 2ND

1864: The first committee for Memorial Tablets, at the Society of Arts, was convened on this day, followed by a first report and recommendations for Memorial Tablets on 9 May. (Society of Arts)

———•◆•———

1892: Sir James Crichton Browne, a leading psychiatrist and one of Charles Darwin's most significant collaborators, delivered a paper today on 'Sex in Education' at the 110th Annual meeting of the London Medical Society. He suggested that expanding education opportunities for women was not in the best interest of their health or their pulchritude. (*The Times*)

———•◆•———

1932: The new headquarters of the BBC, Broadcasting House at Langham Place, entered full service today followed by Sir John Reith's address to his staff in the Concert Hall the next day. It was restored after being bombed twice during the Second World War. (BBC Archives)

May 3rd

1664: Mr Pepys recorded in his diary today that he 'went to Mr Bland's and there drank my morning's draft in chocolate' – London's very first chocolate house was 'in Bishopsgate Street in Queen's Head Alley at a Frenchman's house' in 1657.

1788: Peter Stuart, who edited the *Oracle*, resigned from the *Morning Post* to undertake the issuing of the first regular London evening paper, the *Star and Evening Advertiser*, the first issue of which came out on this day. It became the leading Whig evening paper and was in circulation until 1831.

1951: King George VI inaugurated the Festival of Britain on this day and opened the Royal Festival Hall. (*The Times*)

1960: Mr Wedgwood Ben described the option of paying fixed penalties as 'the mechanization of sin and the automation of absolutions' today in Parliament.

1968: A medical team led by Dr Donald Ross carried out Britain's first heart transplant, on Frederick West at the National Heart Hospital – he died forty-six days later. (*Daily Express*)

MAY 4TH

1847: Jenny Lind, the 'Swedish Nightingale', made her London debut at Her Majesty's Theatre and wowed the audience. (*The Times*)

———•◆•———

1896: The *Daily Mail*, at ½d a copy, devised by Alfred and Harold Harmsworth, was first published on this day. The planned print run of 100,000 for the first day became 397,215!

———•◆•———

1913: The annual exhibition of flowers by the Royal Horticultural Society was held for the first time in the grounds of the Royal Hospital Chelsea. (*The Times*)

———•◆•———

2000: Ken Livingstone, the independent Labour candidate, was elected the first Mayor of London. (*Daily Mail*)

———•◆•———

2008: Boris Johnson, the Conservative candidate for the Mayoralty of London, beat his rival Ken Livingstone and assumed control at City Hall on this day. His candidacy was the object of national and international scrutiny. David Cameron had commented, 'I don't always agree with him, but I respect the fact that he's absolutely his own man'. (*Guardian*)

MAY 5TH

1760: Laurence, Earl Ferrers, was hanged at Tyburn for shooting his steward when drunk. This was the first time a falling trapdoor was used for an execution. His body was then taken to be anatomised. (*Newgate Calendar*)

1840: The seventy-three-year-old Lord William Russell was found stabbed to death at his house in Norfolk Street, WI. Initially thought to be a burglary with violence, his handsome Swiss ex-valet François Courvoisiser was arrested and an eleventh-hour witness sealed his fate. He was hanged at Newgate. (*The Times*)

1897: The Distressed Gentlefolk's Association was founded today by Elizabeth and Constance Finn. It was formed to provide financial aid, and help relieve problems associated with old age. (*The Times*)

1901: Gladstone Park, an 80-acre expanse at Dollis Hill, was opened to the public. (*Willesden Chronicle & Herald*)

1998: On this day the government held a referendum to determine Londoners' views on a new authority for Greater London, headed by an elected mayor; 72 per cent of a 34 per cent turnout voted in favour.

MAY 6TH

1733: The first 'international' boxing match took place at Figg's Amphitheatre in Tottenham Court Road when Bob Whittaker beat a gigantic Italian gondolier, Tito di Carni. (*Capt. Godfrey – a treatise*)

———◆———

1902: This day saw the last hanging at Newgate Prison shortly before it was closed. The apparatus was moved to Pentonville for future use. (Police Annals)

———◆———

1927: On this Friday a trunk was deposited at the left-luggage office at Charing Cross station – it was the dismembered body of Minnie Bonati, murdered by John Robinson. (*Daily Mail*)

———◆———

1960: Princess Margaret wed Mr Anthony Armstrong-Jones at Westminster Abbey on this day – it was the first televised royal wedding, and 300 million people worldwide watched it. (*The Times*)

———◆———

1974: 'The Guitar Player', a painting by Vermeer which was stolen from Kenwood House, was discovered wrapped in paper in the St Bartholomew-the-Great churchyard. (*Evening Standard*)

———◆———

1990: London telephone codes changed to 071 and 081 on this day. (*Evening Standard*)

MAY 7TH

1663: The Theatre Royal Drury Lane, built at the behest of Thomas Killigrew, opened on this day under a Charter by Charles II with a performance of Beaumont and Fletcher's *The Humorous Lieutenant*. Actors who trod the boards here were Nell Gwynne and Charles Hart, amongst others. It burnt down in 1672 and was rebuilt to the designs of Sir Christopher Wren.

———◆———

1849: Lady Blessington and her lover, the Comte d'Orsay, left for France having been served with papers demanding repayment of their massive debts. Today Phillips, the auctioneer, sold her house, Grove House, Kensington, and all its contents. He added, 'the mansion required neither substantial repair nor decorations as very large sums have been lately expended thereon.' (*The Times*)

———◆———

1960: The London Museum showed a reconstruction of an Iron Age settlement found on the site of the BOAC air terminal at Heathrow on this day. (*The Times*)

MAY 8TH

1854: The members of the Athenaeum, a club noted for its scientific members but not for its gastronomy, on this day rebelled against table changes raised to a shilling and the employment of an official carver to slice the beef. A compromise was reached in this Coffee Room Revolt: the shilling price remained for dinner, but luncheon at *6d* … and carving was once again relegated to the amateur. (*The Times*)

1962: The last trolleybus, a large capacity double-decker bus with three axles and rapid acceleration, came off the London roads on this day. (London Transport Museum)

1984: The Thames Flood Barrier, designed as a flood-control system, was opened by Queen Elizabeth II today. The northern bank is in Silvertown and the southern is in the New Charlton area. There have been 114 closures since it opened. (*Sunday Telegraph*)

1993: Millwall Football Club played its last game at the Den in Cold Blow Lane today against Bristol Rovers. It reopened only a few hundred yards away on 4 August. (*Gazette*)

MAY 9TH

1662: The figure of Mr Punch made his first recorded appearance in London today. Samuel Pepys recorded it in a visit to Covent Garden as 'an Italian Puppet Play, that is within the rails there, which is very pretty'. Punch was then called 'Pulcinella'.

1671: Capt. Thomas Blood, an Irish adventurer, disguised himself as a clergyman and with confederates attempted to steal the Crown Jewels from the Tower of London. He failed but was later pardoned by King Charles II. (*Tower History*)

1726: Catherine Hayes was burnt at the stake on this day for petty treason – the killing of a husband by his wife, an assault of the majesty of the state, as well as the actual victim, both perceived to be against the natural order of things. (City of London Records Office)

1885: Police raided the German Anarchist International Club off Rathbone Place, NI, today. A member, Frank Kitz, described the wounds of his colleagues. The police left with jars of beer, money and clothes. (*Slow Burning Fuse*, J. Quail)

MAY 10TH

1737: On this Tuesday a single highwayman robbed four coaches and several passengers at different times on Hounslow Heath 'and they gave out it was Turpin, but that fellow having done so much mischief of late, runs in everybody's head'. (*Social England vol. 5*)

1922: On this Tuesday Ivy Williams was called to the Bar by Henry Dickens. She became the first woman to be called to the English Bar, although she never practised.

1940: As German forces invaded Belgium and Holland, Winston Churchill succeeded as Prime Minister on this day when Neville Chamberlain stood down. Aside from his extraordinary role as war leader, Churchill made a speech in 1946 that recommended a 'United States of Europe'. (*The Times*)

1941: On this Saturday the Luftwaffe attacked London for five hours during the night. The House of Commons was badly hit as were Westminster Abbey, the British Museum, the Law courts and the War Office to a lesser extent; 1,436 people died and 1,792 were injured. (*The Times*)

MAY 11TH

1812: Spencer Perceval, aged forty-nine, the First Lord of the Treasury, entered the lobby of the House of Commons on this sunny Monday afternoon and was shot dead by a merchant, John Bellingham. John Bellingham was hanged at Newgate on 18 May, two days after Perceval's funeral. (*The Times*)

1887: The Earls Court Exhibition Halls were opened to Buffalo Bill's American Exhibition as part of the Jubilee Exhibition. Queen Victoria and her entourage were treated to a private viewing, meeting Annie Oakley the famed sharpshooter, and Red Shirt the Indian chief who had pitched his tepee in South Kensington two weeks before. (*The Times*)

1930: On this day Oswald Mosley, MP and founder of the British Union of Fascists, married Lady Cynthia Curzon in St James's Palace. Whilst married to her, he would have affairs with his mother-in-law and sister-in-law. (*The Times*)

1937: London's 26,000 busmen went on strike on the eve of the Coronation of George VI. They wanted shorter hours, better conditions and an enquiry on the dangers of the new buses. These travelled at 30mph instead of the sedate 12mph they were used to. (*Daily Mail*)

MAY 12TH

1641: Thomas Wentworth, Earl of Strafford, an ardent supporter of Charles I and a political pawn in the power play between his King and Parliament, was attainted for high treason and executed on Tower Hill on this day. His last words were, 'Put not your trust in Princes'. (Guildhall)

1670: On this day the Earl of Bedford was granted the right to regulate a market on every day except Sundays and Christmas day at Covent Garden. Apart from Smithfield, it was the largest market in London. (City of London Records Office)

1891: Capt. Edmund Verney was expelled from the House of Commons on this day. He pleaded guilty to conspiring to procure for corrupt and immoral purposes a girl of nineteen. His crime was made worse as he was a prominent member of the National Vigilance Association, dedicated to the abolition of vice in London. (*The Times*)

1906: The First edition of *John Bull*, a magazine revived by Horatio Bottomley, the Liberal MP and swindler, was published on this day.

MAY 13TH

1790: Mr Abraham Greenwood brought an action against his cousin Mr William Greenwood, bother and heir-at-law of John Greenwood, deceased, who had made a will in favour of Abraham Greenwood. William Greenwood purported his deceased brother to have been of unsound mind – the Jury at Westminster Hall found the deceased sane and the judgment was made in favour of the plaintiff. (Register)

———◆———

1827: Labourers digging for a great new common sewer from Westminster to the Thames on Vauxhall Bridge Road discovered old buckles, shoes and skeletons. This area was called Pest-House Fields because it was used for mass graves during the plague. (Annual Register)

———◆———

1986: Legal history was made on this day by Leo Abse, the MP and solicitor, when he exercised his Right of Audience in the High Court in his professional role – he was the first solicitor able to do so, ending the centuries-old tradition of barristers' monopoly of the High Court. (*The Times*)

MAY 14TH

1842: On this Saturday the *London Illustrated News*, the world's first pictorial weekly newspaper, was born. The first edition had a print run of 26,000 copies and contained some twenty illustrations. By 1851 the circulation had risen to 130,000.

———◆———

1856: The trial of Dr William Palmer, a physician and poisoner, began at the Old Bailey. His victims included his wife, some of his children, his creditors and friends, and his mother-in-law. His initial crime was to live above his means; subsequent attempts were made to swindle insurance companies and friends. (*The Sentinel*)

———◆———

1889: On this day the Revd Benjamin Waugh, a Victorian social reformer and campaigner, founded the London Society for the Prevention of Cruelty to Children launched at the Mansion House. Its patron was Queen Victoria and it evolved to become the NSPCC. (Annual Register)

———◆———

1932: On this day the last transmission was made by the BBC from their Savoy Hill headquarters before wholly transferring to the new Langham Place Headquarters. (BBC)

MAY 15TH

1718: The London lawyer James Puckle patented a revolver type of firearm on this day, patent no. 418. It was, 'a portable gun or machine that discharges so often and so many bullets, and be so quickly loaded as renders it next to impossible to carry any ship by boarding'. The unusually clear drawings showed an early machine gun. His specifications were that round bullets be used on Christians and square ones on Turks. (Patent Office)

———◆———

1855: Three London companies, Abell & Co., Spielmann, and Bull, sent a box of gold bars and coins each, from London Bridge station via the South Eastern Railway to Paris. These weighed 91kg, which would be valued at about £800,000 nowadays.

The boxes were sealed, bound with iron bars and splaced in Chubb-locked safes on a train carriage. On arrival in Paris, the boxes only contained lead. The French authorities claimed that the robbery occurred in England whilst the English said it happened in France. The reality was that it happened between London and Dover – the perpetrators were eventually caught. Michel Crichton wrote a novel about it, *The Great Train Robbery*. (*The Times*)

MAY 16TH

1763: James Boswell was taking tea with Tom Davis, the bookseller at No. 6 Russell Street, when Dr Johnson walked in. Boswell had never met the great man and apologised for being Scottish. Johnson's verbal slap did not deter him. Boswell visited him the following week and the rest is history! (*Boswell's Journal*)

1931: The first London trolleybus ran from this day in the Fulwell–Kingston area, operated by London Tramways. It was nicknamed a Diddler because it resembled a motor bus, and was designed to be a worthy tram replacement, and much quieter. There were eventually a *total* of sixty-eight routes and a fleet of 1,811 trolleybuses. (London Transport Museum)

1968: The Ronan Point Tragedy – a gas explosion on the eighteenth floor of a block of flats in Newham – miraculously only killed four and injured eleven. Public outrage, however, temporarily stalled the building of high-rise flats. (*Daily Mail*)

MAY 17TH

1849: George Hudson, MP and railway entrepreneur, tried on this day in the House of Commons to deny any impropriety as his railway empire collapsed. As an MP he was immune from personal debts, but once unseated he sank into obscurity. Dr John Ainslie and Mr William Jackson bought the lion's share of his defunct empire. (Hansard)

1890: *Comic Cuts*, one of the first weekly comics, was first published today by Alfred Harmsworth of The Associated Press. It first used reprinted comics from the United States, but then went on to spawn a native group of British cartoonists. (Associated Press)

1941: Rudolf Hess, deputy to Adolf Hitler, was the last State prisoner to be held at the Tower of London. He was held there for four days. (*The Times*)

1993: The mile-long Limehouse link to complete the seven-mile Docklands Highway was opened. It cost £345 million and was the most expensive road in Britain. (*The Times*)

MAY 18TH

1827: On this day men, searching under a grain bin in Leadenhall Street, found the shot corpse of Maria Marten. A William Corder had sometime before promised to elope with her. He was discovered, arrested, admitted to his crime and executed. (*The Times*)

———◆———

1921: The erection of a commercial airship mooring-mast, 120ft high, was started on this Wednesday at Croydon Airport. When completed, one of the large rigid-type airships (R33) would be anchored on it for experimental purposes. (*The Times*)

———◆———

1955: A meat patty was named after a character from Popeye, J. Wellington Wimpy, and on this day the first Wimpy opened in a Lyons Corner House in London. It was the first fast-food chain to offer a bean burger in 1985. (*Guardian*)

———◆———

2011: Following a cold case review, two suspects in the Stephen Lawrence murder, Gary Dobson and David Norris, were on this day told that they would stand trial for the murder in light of new and substantial evidence becoming available. (*Daily Mail*)

MAY 19TH

1649: The Rump Parliament passed an Act on this day which created all people of the realm and territories of England a Commonwealth and Free State where Parliament would constitute the officers and ministers of the people without any king or lords. It remained a Republic for eleven years.

1657: The *Publick Advertiser*, devoted entirely to advertising, first appeared in London today with classified advertisements.

1934: On this day a Sherlock Holmes crossword puzzle published in the *Saturday Review of Literature* made whoever solved the puzzle become members of the 'Baker Street Irregulars'.

1958: After a successful tour in the provinces, Harold Pinter's second play *The Birthday Party* opened at the Hammersmith Lyric this Monday to appalling reviews. Production ceased by Saturday, although an exceptionally good review by Harold Hobson turned it and its creator into household names. (*Sunday Times*)

1992: Dave Gander, a former world strongman with a 56in chest, arms measuring 21in in diameter and 33in thighs, pulled a 200-ton Air Canada Boeing 747 jumbo jet 3in at Heathrow. (*Daily Mail*)

MAY 20TH

1715: On this night Randall Lee returned home to find his house broken into, his cellar door smashed open and John Smith, of St Martin in the Fields, smelling of alcohol, clutching a chisel, a lantern and a bunch of matches. The watch was called and at his trial the jury found it hard to believe John Smith's plea of inebriation. They found it easy to find him guilty of burglary and send him to the gallows. (*Newgate Calendar*)

1867: Queen Victoria laid the first stone to the Hall of Arts and Sciences on this day and, despite every effort being made to dissuade her, she renamed it The Royal Albert Hall. (*The Times*)

1913: The Royal Horticultural Society Great Spring Show was forced to relocate from Temple Gardens to the Royal Hospital in Chelsea, in 1912. The venue proved so successful that the RHS Great Spring Show officially started on this day in the same place. It attracted 200,000 visitors and witnessed the arrival of the first Japanese Dwarf Trees, otherwise known as Bonsai. (Royal Horticultural Society)

MAY 21ST

1810: On this day the Chevalier d'Eon de Beaumont died in London. He had been a spy, a diplomat and one of Europe's best swordsmen. He had also dressed as a woman from 1785 and bets were made in London about his sex. A post-mortem revealed he had male genitalia.

———◆◆———

1827: *The Standard* was founded today. It became the dominant evening paper for London.

———◆◆———

1952: Billy Hill's Camden Town Mob on this day made a spectacular robbery in Eastcastle Street, Marylebone. A post-office van filled with used banknotes was ambushed by six men and two cars. It was hijacked and the mob got away with £287,000 – the biggest haul in history at the time. (*Daily Mail*)

———◆◆———

1966: Muhammad Ali beat Henry Cooper in round 6 of a match in London on this day. This shattered Cooper's hopes of Britain winning the World Heavyweight Crown. (*Daily Express*)

MAY 22ND

1896: A Ferris wheel, about 300ft high, was installed at Earls Court in 1895. Ten of the forty cars were furnished with easy chairs and settees for first-class passengers who paid twice the normal fare. Ten of these were for non-smokers. Power was furbished by two 16hp Robey engines. It was hugely popular from the start. The only major incident occurred on this day when it suddenly stopped at around 9 p.m. Most of the passengers spent the night aboard, although seamen from a docked ship scurried around the wheel, taking food and drink to the stranded passengers, and the band of the Grenadier Guards provided music. When the passengers were finally released at 7 a.m. the next morning, they were recompensed with a £5 note each! (*The Times*)

———◆———

1933: The first set of automatic traffic lights to be erected in London, were, seemingly, in Trafalgar Square on 3 April. On this day a second set was erected in Piccadilly Circus. (Annals of London)

MAY 23RD

1701: Capt. William Kidd, a sea captain then privateer, was hanged at Execution Dock, Wapping, on this day, for 'murder and piracy on the high seas'. England was at war with France and he had attacked two Armenian ships sailing under French passes. The French passes which would have exonerated him mysteriously disappeared and have only recently been rediscovered! His body was gibbeted – left to hang in an iron cage over the Thames – for twenty years. (Guildhall)

1905: Alfred and Albert Stratton, brothers, found guilty of the murders of an elderly couple managing a paint shop on Deptford High Street, were on this day hanged at Wandsworth Prison. Their trial was the first in which fingerprints were used as corroborative evidence.

2007: On this day Norbury residents, explained the *Croydon Guardian*, were fighting plans to put storage containers on land used to bury victims of the seventeenth-century Great Plague of London. The Council was rethinking the plan and considering alternatives.

MAY 24TH

1725: Jonathan Wild, a police informer and fence who organised a gang of thieves, became a 'Thief-taker General'. He was eventually convicted of receiving a reward for restoring stolen property and was sentenced to death. He was hanged on this day at Tyburn, to general delight. He was buried in St Pancras but his body was stolen for anatomising. (*Newgate Calendar*)

1738: John Wesley first attended evensong at St Paul's then went to a meeting at Aldersgate where he experienced his conversion. (*Oxford Dictionary of National Biography*)

1871: Frederick Moon, aged forty-one, a wealthy brewer and son of a City alderman, was found stabbed to death in his mistress's flat in Bayswater. 'Mrs' Flora Davy, the mistress, was indicted for murder, for stabbing him when he proposed to end their relationship. Medical opinion prevailed and she was imprisoned for eight years. (*The Times*)

1906: The Ritz Hotel, the creation of César Ritz, was opened on this day. His hotel of the same name in Paris was known the world over. (*The Times*)

MAY 25TH

1722: On or about this date, the Corporation of London decreed that: 'all carts, coaches and all other carriages out of Southwark into this city do keep all along the west side of London Bridge, and all carts and coaches going out of the city do keep along the east side'. This seems to be at the origin of the UK driving on the left-hand side. It was enshrined in Law in the Highways Act of 1835.

1850: Obaysch the hippopotamus arrived in London on this day – the first hippo to reach Europe since the Roman Empire. He proved enormously popular and in 1871 fathered London Zoo's first baby hippo.

1871: The House of Commons passed the Bank Holiday Act on this day, incepted by Sir John Lubbock, creating the public holidays of Easter Monday, Whit Monday and Christmas Day.

1895: Oscar Wilde, the poet-playwright, was today convicted of sodomy at the Old Bailey and sentenced to two years' hard labour. (*The Times*)

MAY 26TH

1868: Michael Barrett, a Fenian responsible for an explosion at Clerkenwell House of Detention in 1867, was the last man to be publicly hanged outside Newgate Prison. (*Newgate Calendar*)

1876: Thomas Gainsborough's exquisite 'Duchess of Devonshire' was stolen from Agnew's Gallery, Bond Street, in the middle of the night. It was described as the most audacious art theft in the world. Agnew's soon received a ransom demand. (*The Times*)

1906: Five years behind schedule, the new Vauxhall Bridge was opened on this day by the Prince of Wales. It was the first London bridge to include tramlines. One of its statues holds the capital's smallest cathedral, a copy of St Paul's. (*The Times*)

1913: Miss Emily Cecilia Duncan served as a Guardian of the West Ham Union for twenty-one years and as Chairman of the West Ham Board of Guardians in 1913-14. She was appointed on this day as the first woman magistrate in the United Kingdom. (*The Times*)

MAY 27TH

1679: Anthony Ashley Cooper, First Earl of Shaftsbury, and one of the first Whigs, instigated the Habeas Corpus Act, which became law on this day. It gives the accused the right to demand on which charge he is being held and to require that he be brought before a court to determine if he is being legally held in custody. This act was incorporated into the American constitution.

———◆———

1541: Margaret Plantagenet, Countess of Salisbury, a frail but indomitable septuagenarian, was beheaded not without difficulty by the inexperienced executioner at the Tower. It took several blows to decapitate her. Her crime was her Plantagenet blood and her son's criticism of Henry VIII's divorce from Catherine of Aragon. (*Oxford Dictionary of National Biography*)

———◆———

1851: The first Chess International Masters tournament was held in London and was won by Adolf Anderssen of Germany. (*The Times*)

MAY 28TH

1741: In front of massed crowds and the Admiral Vernon, Thomas Topham, publican and 'Strong Man of Islington', stood on a platform in Bath Street and lifted, via a rope around his shoulders, three hogsheads of water weighing 11,831lb. (*Daily Gazetteer*)

1742: The first recorded indoor swimming pool, the Bagno, opened in Leman Street on this day. For a guinea, subscription gentlemen could bathe in the 43ft-long pool. Ladies were not permitted. (*Daily Gazetteer*)

1858: Erasmus Bond (1808-1866), mineral-water manufacturer of London, on this day patented tonic water. (Patent Office)

1959: The Mermaid Theatre, the first new theatre in the City of London since 1835, opened in a converted Victorian warehouse. (*The Times*)

1982: On this day Pope John Paul II, the first Roman Catholic pontiff to visit Britain, held a mass at Westminster Cathedral and met the Queen at Buckingham Palace. (*The Times*)

MAY 29TH

1585: An ordinance issued on this day granted Westminster its own laws and constitution – the new municipality would dramatically expand in the next fifty years. (Westminster City Archives)

———•———

1660: The good-natured Charles II made a triumphant entry into London, saluted by over 20,000 troops. (John Evelyn)

———•———

1743: On this day John Wesley opened a chapel in West Street off Charing Cross Road, formerly a Huguenot Chapel. This remained the headquarters of Methodist work in the West End until 1798. (*Oxford Dictionary of National Biography*)

———•———

1884: On this day at the church of St James, Paddington, Oscar Wilde, an impecunious poet-playwright, married Constance Lloyd. He quipped that he had told Queen Victoria that 'in this weather I asked her to remain at Osborne'.

———•———

1922: MP Horatio Bottomley was on this day sentenced to seven years for fraud. His 'Victory bonds' had attracted money from thousands of small investors and netted him £150,000. (*The Times*)

———•———

2002: Paul Boateng became the first black Cabinet minister when he was appointed Chief Secretary to the Treasury on this day. (*The Times*)

MAY 30TH

1726: On this Whit Monday François Marie Arouet, better known as Voltaire, set foot on English soil at Greenwich. 'I fancied I was transported to the Elysean Fields, but the beauty of the Thames, the crowd of vessels and the vast size of the City of London soon made me blush to have likened Elys to England'. (*Memoires*)

1842: Queen Victoria and her consort were used as bait when they went on a carriage ride on Constitution Hill on this day. A man had previously been seen levelling a gun at the Royal Landau. He did indeed reappear. He pulled the trigger and was seized – no one was harmed. A woman heard him say, 'Damn the Queen – why should she be such an expense to the nation?' (*The Times*)

1884: On his day by 9 p.m. the CID and the Special Irish Branch headquarters were successfully bombed by the Fenians. The bomb was concealed in a cast-iron urinal on the corner of a detached building in the centre of Scotland Yard. (Police Archives)

MAY 31ST

1718: John Price, public hangman, was hanged for the murder of Elizabeth White, in Bunhill Fields. (*Newgate Calendar*)

1810: At 2.30 a.m. the Duke of Cumberland, sleeping in his bed in St James Palace, was attacked. His assailant's blade hacked through the duke's padded nightgown. Woken, he fought off his attacker and cried for help. By the time a valet appeared, the interloper had fled. (*The Times*)

1856: Prince Albert laid the foundation stone of a Home for Asiatics, Africans, South Sea Islanders and others occasionally residing in the Metropolis. The home was in West India Road, near the church of St Andrew's, Limehouse. (*The Times*)

1946: Heathrow Airport superseded Croydon as the civil airport for London. Ambitious plans for the extension of this airport ensured that within four years the villages of Sipson and Harlington, 1,200 houses, four schools, and twelve pubs disappeared. (*The Times*)

JUNE 1ST

1593: Christopher Marlowe was 'slain by Francis Archer' at a house in Deptford. The poet, playwright, secret agent and atheist was supposedly drunk. (Sheriff's written evidence)

1664: 'With my wife to take ayres, it being very warm and pleasant, to bowe and Olde Forde and thence to Hackney. There light and played at shuffleboard, eat cream and good cherries and so with good refreshment home.' (Pepys)

1783: Charles Byrne (1761-1783), an Irish giant said to have been 8ft 4in and tall enough to light his pipe from a street lamp, died on this day in London of tuberculosis and the ravages of alcohol. He had made and lost several fortunes as a freak in the provinces and London through mismanagement and irresponsible and criminal managers. His one fear when he died was that his body would be sold to surgeons to be anatomised. Despite all precautions being taken, Resurrectionists stole his body from his coffin on the way to Margate and sold it to the surgeon John Hunter. (*Evening Standard*)

JUNE 2ND

1216: Louis 'The Lion', Dauphin of France entered London on this day to a rapturous reception. Twelve of the country's twenty bishops welcomed him, as did the Mayor. He processed triumphantly into St Paul's Cathedral and swore on the gospels that he would restore to his new vassals all their rightful inheritances and good laws. (*Blood Cries Afar*, Sean McGlynn)

1780: On this Friday Henry Angelo, director of a Fencing Academy, noted that 'five thousand rabble went over the bridge to the House of Commons, I hastened to Parliament Street ... a great throng shouting *No Popery* ... In the evening from the window of a house in Queen Street Long Acre, I saw and counted ten fires blazing in the middle of the street to burn those whom the mob called *Papishes*'.

1938: Robert and Edward Kennedy, sons of the US Ambassador, opened Regent's Park Children's Zoo. (*The Times*)

1953: Today the Coronation of Elizabeth II as Queen was performed at Westminster Abbey. There were 8,000 guests, 3 million onlookers and 20 million television viewers. (*Daily Telegraph*)

JUNE 3RD

1819: *The Times* reported on this day that the Italian library run by Mr Zolti was open to anyone desirous of increasing their knowledge of Italy and Italian art and literature.

1831: The violinist Nicolo Paganini was mobbed on the streets of London on his first visit when he performed at the King's Theatre. (*The Times*)

1837: A Notting Hill entrepreneur, John Whyte, leased 200 acres of James Weller Ladbroke's land bounded by the Portobello and Pottery Lanes to the east and west, Notting Hill Terrace (Ladbroke Road) to the south and Lancaster road to the north – and on this he built a hippodrome which opened on this day. It lasted until 1843. (*The Times*)

1843: Lola Montez made her London debut at Her Majesty's Theatre on this day. Despite her success she was recognised as Mrs James, originally Eliza Gilbert, an Irish adventuress. 'La Grande Horizontale', as she was known, was immensely successful in her chosen sphere. (*The Times*)

JUNE 4TH

1456: Soon after the anti-alien riots of May, quite probably on this day, what has subsequently been identified as Halley's Comet appeared in the London sky. (City of London Records Office)

—•—

1807: Frederick Winser, an expatriate German, followed his gas-lighting of Pall Mall with a special exhibition on this day, in honour of the birthday of King George III, using gaslight to superimpose images against the walls of the buildings along his street. (*The Times*)

—•—

1940: Winston Churchill made his rousing speech on this day in London: 'We shall go on to the end ... We shall fight in France ... We shall fight on the beaches ...We shall never surrender'. It was a defining moment in the war and was based on the French President Georges Clemenceau's speech half a century earlier.

—•—

2002: The Golden Jubilee celebrations of Queen Elizabeth II were attended by thousands of people in London, despite the *Guardian* predicting that this event would be a wash-out.

JUNE 5TH

1886: In a match between Blackheath Cricket Club and a gentleman's touring team called the Band of Brothers led by Lord Harris, Montague Druitt bowled Harris for 14 and took three wickets. Two weeks later, Druitt dismissed England's batsman, John Shuter, who was playing for Bexley Cricket Club, for a duck, and Blackheath won the game by 114 runs.

Druitt's corpse was found floating by Chiswick on the Thames in 1888. It seems he had committed suicide. Druitt was long considered a profile match for 'Jack the Ripper'.

1929: Margaret Bondfield, Trade Unionist, women's campaigner and MP, became the first woman to be a minister, under Ramsay Macdonald, as Minister for Labour, and first woman to become a Privy Councillor. (*The Times*)

1963: John Profumo resigned as Secretary for War after admitting he had lied over his affair with Christine Keeler. (*Daily Mail*)

JUNE 6TH

1523: The Emperor Charles V of Spain, on a visit to London to persuade Henry VIII to support him against France, proceeded with Henry VIII from Greenwich Palace to Blackfriars in regal splendour. (Stow)

———•◆•———

1585: On this day, or thereabouts, a school for thieves was discovered in Billingsgate. A pocket and purse guarded by a bell would sound if touched by a clumsy thief. A pickpocket was called a 'foyster' and a cut-purse a 'nypper'. (Stow)

———•◆•———

1727: Today the King's Theatre was a tumult with crowds round the doors throwing insults and punches at supporters on either side; even the singers fought on stage. (*Daily Courant*)

———•◆•———

1858: On this day, a curate of St Barnabas, Knightsbridge, the Revd Alfred Poole, was suspended from office for practising auricular confession. (*The Times*)

———•◆•———

1922: *Child Whispers*, Enid Blyton's first book, was published today by Dean & Son. It was written whilst she was governess to the four children of Mr and Mrs Thompson at No. 207 Hook Road, Chessington.

JUNE 7TH

1566: The first stone was laid for the Royal Exchange building. The architect, much to Londoners' disgust, was foreign, as were many of the workers. (*Haydn's Dictionary*)

1567: A census of foreigners in the City found that there were '40 Scots, 428 Frenchmen, 45 Spaniards, 140 Italians, 2,030 Dutch, 44 Burgundians, 2 Danes and 1 Liegeois' on this day. (*Haydn's Dictionary*)

1695: On this day the *Postboy* newspaper reported that gentlemen were affronted by masked Hackney coach drivers in the Ring in Hyde Park. The Lord Justice ordered that no hackney coaches be permitted in the said area. This ban lasted until the 1920s.

2003: Just after 6:30 p.m. a flash mob of 200 people summoned by the internet descended on the Sofa UK store off Tottenham Court Road. The instructions were to appreciate the furniture on show and then ring a friend on a mobile and talk about it without using the letter 'O'. (*Evening Standard*)

JUNE 8TH

1841: On this Tuesday at about 4.30 a.m., Astley's Theatre, at the foot of Westminster Bridge, caught fire. At the time the fire broke out there were about fifty horses in the establishment as well as two zebras and some asses. Most of the horses were rescued. Some of the local houses burnt down but there was no loss of life. Mr Ducrow and his family escaped unharmed. (*The Times*)

———◆———

1925: Noel Coward's comedy *Hay Fever* opened, making theatrical history as there were then three Coward plays running concurrently in the West End. The other two were *The Vortex* and *Fallen Angels*. (*Variety*)

———◆———

1968: James Earl Ray was arrested at Heathrow today, travelling under an assumed name and with a false passport, on charges of conspiracy and murder in connection with the assassination of the Civil Rights leader Dr Martin Luther King Jr. (*Daily Mail*)

JUNE 9TH

1873: The recently opened Alexandra Palace caught fire at about 1 p.m. – the three domes caught fire in less than twenty minutes. The falling roof spread the flames before even any water hydrants could be turned on. The whole building was gutted by 2.30 p.m. (*Manchester Guardian*)

———•———

1888: The *East London Observer* printed an article about the twenty-three-year-old George Neighbour, who was charged with breaking and entering No. 11 Hooper Street, Leman Street, Whitechapel, and stealing therefrom a large number of articles belonging to the tenants.

———•———

1978: The Gutenberg Bible, the first book printed on a mechanical press and the first major work to be printed with moveable type, marked the start of a printing revolution. Less than fifty copies now survive. On this day one was sold by private treatise in London to the University of Texas for over £1 million. (*The Times*)

JUNE 10TH

1215: On this day the City of London was granted a Charter by King John, that it would have 'all its ancient liberties by land as well as by water'. (Stow)

— ◆ —

1845: New Oxford Street, connecting Oxford Street to Holborn, was opened to carriages on this day. It was cut across a maze of streets which included the infamous St Giles Rookery, described in vivid detail by Mayhew and Booth. These local slums disappeared, apart from two streets, Church Lane and Carrier Street. (*Standard*)

— ◆ —

1948: Three female patients aged between eleven and twenty-three had operations on this day at Guy's Hospital to unblock valves in their heart. They were known collectively as the 'Blue Babies' as they had a blue hue from birth because of the lack of oxygen in their blood. This was the first heart operation of its kind. (*The Times*)

— ◆ —

2000: The pedestrian-only Millennium Bridge opened on this day and began to wobble alarmingly. It was closed for two years to enable engineers to solve the problem. (*Daily Mail*)

JUNE 11TH

1763: The thirty-eight-year old Giacomo Arrighi de Casanova, a Venetian whose amorous intrigues fascinate to this day, arrived in London today to rekindle old flames with the redoubtable Mrs Cornelys, light new flames and start a harem in Pall Mall. His unadvised dalliance with the mistress of a Livonian Baron made him leave abruptly on 11 March 1764. (*Memoirs; Casanova*)

———◆———

1819: On this Friday Mr Mortimer sent a girl who was caring for his infant child to collect two of his other children from school. She took the infant and on the way met a woman whom she knew, who accompanied her. On her return with the children, the woman asked the girl to get something from a grocer's in Rathbone Place while she looked after the infant and children. The woman sent the children after her. Her purchase done, the girl found the woman and child gone. (*The Times*)

———◆———

1862: The closure of a halfway house for 'fallen women' due to lack of funds forced the St Marylebone Female Protection Society of No. 157 Marylebone Road to make an appeal for funds on this day. (*The Times*)

JUNE 12TH

1381: The Kent insurgents of the Peasants' Revolt, an uprising that stemmed from the taxes imposed on the working population for the wars against France and a growing despondency against the feudal system, arrived today at Blackheath, headed by Wat Tyler, and encamped there.

———◆———

1599: Steve Sohner, the Shakespeare scholar, argues that this was the day that Richard Burbage's Globe was opened on Giles Allen's land near where the present Globe is built.

———◆———

1987: Margaret Thatcher was elected for a third term on this day. She beat Labour by 276 to 229 seats. She was the first Prime Minister in 160 years to win three successive terms of office. This was also the first time black people were elected to Parliament.

———◆———

1997: Largely due to the untiring efforts of the American director and actor, Sam Wanamaker, the modern Shakespeare's Globe Theatre, sited not 230m from the original site, was opened on this day. (*The Times*)

JUNE 13TH

1732: On this day John Waller, an informant convicted of perjury, was pilloried at Seven Dials, a trial he would die of. (City of London Records Office)

1790: Anne Porter, a previous victim of a sadistic attacker nicknamed the London Monster, recognised him in St James Park. Her beau followed Rhynwck Williams and, despite protestations, Williams was charged with defacing someone's clothing. He was sentenced to six years in prison on this day. (*Morning Post*)

1842: Queen Victoria's train ride from Windsor to Paddington, a journey she did not much enjoy, gave greater impetus to the nascent railway-building mania. (*The Times*)

1886: Henry J. Heinz, an American businessman, visited Fortnum & Mason of Piccadilly on this day and on the 16th. He sold his consignment of baked beans and was to sell Fortnum & Mason his tomato soup in 1910. (Fortnum & Mason Archives)

1944: The first V1 Rocket, a pulse-jet powered unmanned aircraft, reached London early this morning and hit Grove Road in Mile End. (*Daily Telegraph*)

JUNE 14TH

1381: On this Friday the fourteen-year-old Richard II, King of England, met the leaders of the Peasants' Revolt – Wat Tyler, Jack Straw and John Ball – at Mile End, and agreed to their demands, namely the abolition of serfdom.

———◆·———

1729: It was reported on this day that one 'Everet of Fleet Lane sold his wife to one Griffin of Long Lane for a 3s bowl of punch, who we hear hath since complained of having a bad bargain'. (City of London Records Office)

———◆·———

1822: Charles Babbage, son of a Walworth banker, a mathematician, philosopher, inventor and mechanical engineer, on this day proposed, in a paper to the Astronomical Society in Bedford Street, a difference engine – an automatic mechanical calculator. The paper was entitled 'Note on the Application of Machinery to the computation of astronomical and mathematical tables' – in short, the precursor of the computer. (*Oxford Dictionary of National Biography*)

JUNE 15TH

1574: On this day at Greenwich, Queen Elizabeth enacted the Statutes of Apparel, requesting, 'That all manner of persons in all places to reform their apparel … none shall wear any silk of the colour purple, cloth of gold, tissued, nor fur of sables, but only the King, Queen …'.

———•———

1825: The foundation stone of the New London Bridge was laid by John Garratt, Lord Mayor and Alderman of Bridge within in the presence of the Duke of York. It had been designed by John Rennie and major new approach roads had to be built to accommodate it. The old bridge continued to be used until it was finished in 1831. (City of London Records Office)

———•———

2011: Harrods, sold to the Qataris by Mohamed Al Fayed, started selling super yachts on this day. The Mars model, according to *The Times*, was the most expensive, retailing at £100 million.

JUNE 16TH

1670: 'I was forced to accompany some friends to the Bear Garden; where was cock fighting, bear, dog-fighting, bear and bull-baiting, it being a famous day for all these butcherly sports, or rather barbarous cruelties'. (*John Evelyn's Diary*)

1737: At about midday Robert Long of Limehouse went out. Returning in the evening, he found his wife dead with her throat cut and his child's neck broken. Both had also had their heads smashed with a hammer. (City of London Records Office)

1819: The *Morning Post* reported that Monsieur, Madame and Mademoiselle Saqui would go through surprising evolutions at Vauxhall. At the end of the ascent, Mme Saqui would make an astonishing ascent on the tightrope amidst a brilliant display of fireworks.

1824: The MP Richard Martin, William Wilberforce and others met at the Old Slaughter's Coffee House by Covent Garden to found a society dedicated to the prevention of the mistreatment of animals. In 1840 Queen Victoria granted them a Charter. (RSPCA Archives)

JUNE 17TH

1497: King Henry VII and an army of 25,000 decisively beat an ill-equipped army of Cornishmen at Deptford Bridge adjacent to the Ravensbourne River. It was the culminating event of the Cornish Rebellion against a tax levy for war to raise money for a campaign against Scotland.

1717: 'On this Wednesday evening the King took water at Whitehall in an open Barge ... and went up river towards Chelsea. Many other barges with persons of quality attended, and so a great number of boats that the whole river in a manner was covered; a City company's barge was employed for the Musick, wherein were 50 instruments of all sorts, who play'd all the way from Lambeth ... the finest symphonies compos'd express for this occasion by Mr Hendel.' (*Daily Courant*)

1789: Henry Angelo, Master at Arms and director of a Fencing Academy, wrote in his diary that on this day 'at about eight o'clock when in Berkeley Square I saw black smoke ascending ... I beheld The Opera House in Drury Lane in flames'.

JUNE 18TH

1583: Richard Martin, an alderman of the City of London, on this day arranged an insurance policy for William Gibbons, a salter. The premium was 8 per cent; the term was eight months. It was the first known insurance policy. (City of London Records Office)

———◆◆———

1746: Today Samuel Johnson contracted with several London publishers, William Strahan, Thomas Longman and Robert Dodsley, to produce a complete dictionary of the English Language. He would be paid 1,500 guineas but no royalties. (City of London Records Office)

———◆◆———

1940: At Studio B2 of the BBC, Brig.-Gen. Charles De Gaulle addressed all the French, inviting them to join him in England to continue the struggle: 'Whatever happens the flame of French resistance will not extinguish nor be extinguished.' This call to arms was, however, never aired, but a second version was quickly printed and distributed in London. (BBC)

———◆◆———

1999: Urban Dream Capsule, four shaven-headed Australian actors, spent two weeks in the Arding & Hobbs windows in Clapham Junction. Apart from toilet facilities, every inch of every room in the 'set' was open to public scrutiny. This formed part of the International Festival of Theatre. (*Daily Mirror*)

JUNE 19TH

1821: George IV was crowned on this day at Westminster Abbey. 'Prinny' had led a life of excess until he was told that if he wanted any more money he would need to marry and produce an heir. The unattractive and forthright Caroline of Brunswick produced him a child that died. The then Prince Regent informed her then that he no longer wanted to have anything to do with her. The spurned queen did as she wanted, and more. Attempts to have the marriage annulled proved fruitless, and when George was crowned she was told that she would not be taking part in the ceremony and was refused entrance.

———•◆•———

1955: The Automobile Association, as a climax to their Golden Jubilee celebrations, presented a cavalcade of motoring history in Regent's Park on this Sunday. (*The Times*)

———•◆•———

1960: Nan Winton, an experienced journalist, on this day began a job reading the 6 p.m. news and weekend bulletins on Sunday evenings. BBC audience research concluded that viewers thought that a woman reading the 'Late News' was 'not acceptable' and so she was removed in March 1961. (BBC)

June 20th

1837: Queen Victoria acceded to the throne on this day on the death of her uncle, King William IV.

1843: Edward Drummond, Peel's Private Secretary, was fatally shot in the back, in Parliament Street, by the deranged Daniel McNaughton. McNaughton's subsequent arrest, trial and institutionalisation for life led to the creation of McNaughton's Rules – 'Nothing is an offence when done by a person who, by reason of unsoundness of mind, is incapable of knowing the nature of the act or that he is doing what is either wrong or contrary to the law.'

1955: The Fulham Housing Committee put into place a plan for a curfew for children on the estates. Young children would be discouraged from playing outside by 7:30 p.m. in the winter and 9 p.m. in the summer. Parents were overwhelmingly in favour. (*The Times*)

1955: The trial began on this day at the Old Bailey of Mrs Ruth Ellis, who was accused of the murder of David Blakely outside the Magdala Tavern in South Hill Park, Hampstead, on 10 April. She was found guilty and sentenced to hang.

June 21st

1675: On this day Master Mason Thomas Strong laid the first stone for the new St Paul's Cathedral, Sir Christopher Wren's masterpiece. He and his brother Edward worked for Wren on other buildings, namely the lodgings of Trinity College and Wadham College Oxford. It would be twenty-two years before divine service was performed in the new building. A tablet in Strong's honour and to those who helped build this edifice was erected by the Worshipful Company of Masons. (City of London Records Office)

———◆———

1819: On this Monday afternoon Mr Brotherhood, a surgeon of Soho, agitatedly walked to the front door of Mr Donaldson, a broker at Castle Court, the Strand. Finding the door shut, he took a lancet out of his pocket and cut his neck from ear to ear. Despite assistance being brought forthwith, he bled to death there. (*The Times*)

———◆———

1937: The Wimbledon Tennis Championships were televised for the first time on this day when matches were transmitted by the BBC from Centre Court for up to half-an-hour each day.

JUNE 22ND

1814: The first match played at Lord's Cricket Ground was between Marylebone Cricket Club and Hertfordshire on this day. The MCC won by an innings and 27 runs.

1948: The first large group of Caribbeans following the war, nearly 500 of them, arrived on this day on the *Empire Windrush* and were housed in Clapham South Deep Shelter as a temporary measure. The *Daily Express* reported: 'All of them sat down to their first meal on English soil: roast beef, potatoes, vegetables, Yorkshire pudding, suet pudding with currants and custard.' The report continued '...a bed and three hot meals cost them *6s 6d* (33p) a day. Most of the Jamaicans have about £5 to last them until they find work.'

1953: Reginald Christie was tried for the murder of his wife at No. 10 Rillington Place, Notting Hill. He had previously admitted to seven murders, and several corpses in various stages of decomposition had been found in the house garden and shed. He had also killed Beryl Evans and her daughter. He was found guilty after a four-day trial and was hanged on 15 July. (*Daily Mail*)

JUNE 23RD

1722: The *London Journal* commented that: 'Boxing in publick at the Bear Garden is what hath lately obtained very much amongst men, but till last week we never heard of women being engaged in that way, when two of the feminine gender appeared for the first time on the theatre of War at Hockley in the Hole.'

1775: On this Friday a regatta filled the river with all vessels from London Bridge to the Ship Tavern at Millbank; 2,000 of the Quality descended on Ranelagh Gardens for a supper organised by Mrs Cornelys. (*Public Advertiser*)

1940: On this day Terry Nelhams-Wright was born at No. 4 Churchfield Road, Acton. He began his musical career in 1957 and was noticed by Jack Good, a producer, who rebranded him as 'Adam Faith', a combination of two Oxford friends of Good's names – Adam Fremantle and Nicholas Faith. Adam Faith became one of the most charted acts of the 1960s and was the first UK artist to lodge his first initial seven hits in the Top 5. (*Daily Mail*)

JUNE 24TH

1699: A committee of London Jews under the direction of Rabbi David Nieto leased land at Plough Yard, in Bevis Marks, from Lady Ann Poyntz and Sir Thomas Poyntz. Prior to this, the committee had engaged a builder, Joseph Avis , a Quaker, to construct a building. This was the beginning of the oldest house of worship of the Ashkenazi Jews in London, the Bevis Marks synagogue. Prior to this, the community had met in a synagogue in Cree Street, but the considerable influx of Jews made it necessary to obtain more commodious quarters. (*Jewish Dictionary*)

———◆———

1830: The last person who stood in the pillory of London, at the Old Bailey, was Peter James Bossy, tried for perjury and sentenced to transportation for seven years. Prior to transportation he was to be kept for six months in Newgate, and to stand for one hour in the pillory at the Old Bailey. The pillory part of the sentence was executed on this day. Another punishment for perjury was being sentenced to ride from Newgate to Cornhill with paper mitres on their heads. (*Old and New London*, E. Walford)

JUNE 25TH

1303: On this day John Droxford, Keeper of the King's Wardrobe, arrested Richard of Pudlicott for the theft of divers' silver plates and treasure from the King's Wardrobe in the chapter house of Westminster Abbey. The theft had taken place when the King and his people had been removed to York for over five years. On or about 24 March, Pudlicott, a merchant bankrupted by King Edward's exigencies, had, with the assistance of at least twelve others, robbed the Wardrobe. He was eventually executed and several monks were admonished. (*Inventories of the Exchequer*)

———◆———

1756: On this day Jonas Hanway called a meeting of merchants to recruit men for the Royal Navy by providing them with clothing kits. The resulting Marine Society proved the most sustained and most successful of its kind. (City of London Records Office)

———◆———

2005: A passer-by noticed a person huddled on a crane counterweight 130ft from the ground at 1.30 a.m. near Dulwich. Once the police and fire service were called it was established that the fifteen-year-old girl had slept-walked from her home. It took a call from her parents to wake her up. (*Daily Mail*)

JUNE 26TH

1819: Dr Johnson had lived at No. 8 Bolt Court, off Fleet Street, from 1776-1784, and on this day this house which had survived a blaze in 1807 was completely gutted by fire. (*The Times*)

———◆———

1846: On this day the repeal of the Corn Law, a law that stopped the foreign import of corn to protect the native industry, led to rioting in the London streets. (*The Times*)

———◆———

1857: The first investiture of the Victoria Cross by Queen Victoria took place in Hyde Park on this Friday. Sixty-two Crimean veterans had the cross pinned on by the monarch. (*The Times*)

———◆———

1868: By today a Blue Plaque to Napoleon III had been affixed at 1c King Street, SW1. It was the first 'Blue' Plaque to be erected and the first plaque to survive. The plaques made by Minton Hollins were originally brown, but blue became the norm. (Society of Arts)

JUNE 27TH

1556: On this day 20,000 people watched the burning at stake of eleven Protestant men and women for heresy. These martyrs, Henry Adlington, Thomas Bowyer, Lyon Cawch, John Derisall, Agnes George, William Hallywell, Edmund Hurst, Ralph Jackson, Lawrence Parnam, Elizabeth Pepper, John Routh, George Searles and Henry Wye, had a memorial erected to them at St John's church, Stratford, in 1879.

1776: The former Royal chaplain and forger, Dr William Dodd, a high-living curate who had forged a cheque, was trundled from Newgate Prison to Tyburn in driving rain where he was hanged for fraud. (*Newgate Calendar*)

1967: The actor Reg Varney unveiled the world's first automated Teller Machine (ATM) at Barclay's Bank, Church Street, Enfield. (*Daily Mail*)

1971: Gyles Brandreth placed a small ad in *The Times* inviting anyone interested in taking part in a National Scrabble Championship to contact him. He received over 3,000 replies and, after contacting J.W. Spears, the then owners of the game, the Championships were born. The first took place on this day in London and was won by an unemployed lecturer, Stephen Haskell. (*Daily Mail*)

JUNE 28TH

1830: PC Joseph Grantham, intervening in a disturbance in the Somers Town area of Euston, was kicked in the head by a drunk and suffered a fatal brain haemorrhage. A jury ruled that it was justifiable homicide as the officer was 'over-exerting' in his line of duty. (Police Records)

1838: The eighteen-year-old Victoria was crowned at Westminster Abbey on this day. The crowds gathered from Palace to Abbey, moving the young Queen to write later of how encouraging they had been. The long ceremony was enlivened by the aged Lord Rollo living up to his name when he stumbled and rolled down some steps; and the Archbishop of Canterbury getting the ring, designed for Victoria's little finger, stuck on the wrong digit. Victoria would be the longest reigning British monarch until the twenty-first century. (*The Times*)

1994: On this day McDonald's sued two members of Greenpeace for an alleged libel in pamphlets. This became the longest civil or criminal case in British legal history. (*The Times*)

JUNE 29TH

1650: Henry Robinson, a writer, established an office of 'Addresses and Encounters' in Threadneedle Street on this day. Clients could have legal advice for a fee, servants were matched to potential employers' needs, and matrimonial affairs were managed. (*Dictionary of National Biography*)

———•———

1893: On this day the Duke of Westminster presided over a distinguished company to unveil the fountain and statue of Anteros, also called the Angel of Christian Charity, or nowadays 'Eros'. He 'unveiled the fountain, and the Duchess of Westminster set the fountains in motion and, amid cheers drank the first cup of water from them'. Sir Harry Verney said, 'I think this fountain is remarkably well designed, and it is a remarkably suitable memorial to Lord Shaftesbury, for it is always giving water to rich and poor alike at all times of day and night.' (*The Times*)

———•———

1901: On this day the Horniman Museum was opened to the public: a collection of marvels from many lands collected by a member of the Horniman family. (*Illustrated London News*)

———•———

1920: Croydon Airport replaced Hounslow Airport as London's civil Airport. (*The Times*)

JUNE 30TH

1604: During an argument at the House of Commons, a young Jackdaw flew into the House and was seen as a portent of evil on a proposed Bill. (*London Register*)

———•◆•———

1894: Tower Bridge was officially opened on this day by the Prince of Wales (the future King Edward VII) and his wife, Alexandra of Denmark. Construction started in 1886 and took eight years, and five major contractors, to finish. The original brick façade was replaced with the more ornate Victorian Gothic style. This makes the bridge a distinctive landmark and harmonises with the nearby Tower of London. Because it is a bascule bridge, with moveable arms to enable tall boats to pass, it is insured as a ship. (*The Times*)

July 1st

1506: A Royal ordinance, on or about this day, suppressed the 'Stews' or brothels of Southwark, but twelve of the eighteen were allowed to reopen shortly afterwards. (City of London Records Office)

1593: On this day a very large-scale Irish immigration was recorded, notably at Wapping and St Giles in the Fields. They were regarded with suspicion – because they were Catholic. (City of London Records Office)

1627: On this day Latymer School began in a building in Fulham churchyard. This bequest of Edward Latymer was to move to Hammersmith in 1648.

1681: Oliver Plunkett, a Roman Catholic priest, became the last Roman Catholic martyr to die in England when he was hanged, drawn and quartered.

1838: At a meeting at the Linnean Society of London today, papers from Charles Darwin and Alfred Russell Wallace were presented that outlined the theory of evolution by natural selection. (Linnean Society)

JULY 2ND

1462: A new spire for St Paul's was completed but the weathercock proved a disaster – 'Robert Godwin, winding it up, the rope brake and he was destroyed on the pinnacles, and the cock was sore-bruised'. (Stow)

1900: Austin Reed, aged twenty-seven, the son of a hosier and hatter, opened a gents outfitters in Fenchurch Street on this day. By 1908 he had three shops in the City, and a branch in Regent Street opened in 1911. (Oxford Dictionary of National Biography)

1953: John Beckley and his friend Matthew Chandler made some remarks within earshot of a gang of Teddy Boys at Clapham Common Bandstand. These gave chase, dragged the two off a bus and stabbed Beckley to death. A lengthy hunt ended with John Michael Davies being arrested, tried and condemned to death, but reprieved. The shame was the reluctance of the fifty bus passengers who witnessed the attack to give evidence. (*Mirror*)

July 3rd

1322: On this day 300 men and women were crushed to death in a rush to beg food and money at the gate of Black Friars Priory. (City of London Records Office)

———•◆•———

1877: William Gibbs, a scholar of Bluecoats School, aged twelve, strangled himself while locked up for running away this night. An investigative committee later exonerated the authorities. (*The Times*)

———•◆•———

1935: Designed by J.H. Markham, the Geological Museum at South Kensington was opened on this day. It was originally derived from a Museum of Economic Geology based in Whitehall.

———•◆•———

1996: It was announced in the House of Commons on this day, due in part to the growing dissatisfaction among Scots at the prevailing constitutional settlement, that the Stone of Scone would be returned to Scotland. The handover was made on St Andrew's Day.

July 4th

1829: George Shillibeer established London's first regular omnibus service on this day; his horse-drawn coaches ran daily from Paddington, via Regent's Street Park to Bank in the City, carrying up to twenty passengers. (*Morning Post*)

1833: 'Sale of a wife'; on this Tuesday at 2 p.m. at Portman market, 'the husband accompanied by his wife with a halter round her neck … the first bidding was 4*s*, the next 4*s* 6*d* … A dustman carried her off amidst the hisses of the crowd for 5*s*'. (*Morning Post*)

1848: The Roman Catholic church of St George was solemnly opened on this day by Bishop (later Cardinal) Wiseman. It was consecrated as a cathedral in 1894. (*The Times*)

1876: The Lincoln Tower, along with Christchurch and ancillary buildings, located at the corner of Westminster Bridge Road and Kennington Park Road, was opened today. It was the brainchild of C.N. Hall who raised funds in America for a permanent memorial to Abraham Lincoln and the abolition of slavery. (*The Times*)

JULY 5TH

1764: Daniel Mendoza, the first Jewish British boxer, was born in Aldgate on this day (although Jewish records suggest 1765). He developed what could be termed as the modern way of boxing, 'Ducking and diving', and moving around. He became boxing champion of England from 1792-95 and was so popular that the London press reported news of his bouts before that of the storming of the Bastille. (*Oxford Dictionary of National Biography*)

1805: Jerome Napoleon Bonaparte, son of Prince Jerome Bonaparte and the American Elizabeth Patterson, was born on this day at No. 95 Camberwell Grove, Camberwell. His mother took him back to America shortly afterwards and his parents' marriage was annulled by order of the Emperor.

1969: The Rolling Stones gave a free concert to 250,000 fans in Hyde Park on this day, following the death of the group's guitarists Brian Jones two days earlier. (*Daily Mail*)

JULY 6TH

1535: Former Lord Chancellor Thomas More was executed for high treason on this day for refusing to take the Oath of Supremacy. (*Oxford Dictionary of National Biography*)

1551: Henry Machyn recorded that a 'swet [sweating sickness] began in London on this day which carried off many people both noble and commoners'. The King, though, retired to Hampton Court.

1746: Charles Lilly, the perfumer with a shop at the corner of the Beaufort Buildings in the Strand, was buried at St Mary's, Finchley, on this day. In 1708 he had introduced scented snuffs and a revolutionary fragrance consisting of orange flower, musk, civet, violet and amber. He also achieved posthumous fame when his encyclopaedia on perfumes was published in 1822. (Burial records)

1892: Dadabhai Naoroji became, on this day, the first Asian to be elected to the House of Commons, as Liberal MP for Finsbury Central. (*Liberal Dictionary*)

2005: On this day Trafalgar Square witnessed thousands of people in jubilation over Britain winning the contest to host the Olympic Games in 2012. (*Evening Standard*)

JULY 7TH

1783: John Austin, a forger, was the last person to be hanged publicly at Tyburn Tree. (City of London Records Office)

———◆———

1792: At 8 a.m. on this Sunday, Brigadier Benjamin Arnold fought a pistol duel with Lord Lauderdale at Kilburn Wells (just off Kilburn High Street). Lauderdale later apologised for besmirching the Brigadier. (*Dictionary of Canadian Biography*)

———◆———

1888: On this day 1,400 girls making matches at the Bryant & May factory in Fairfield Row, Bow, went on strike. Poor working conditions, twelve-hour working days and the cavalier dismissal of one worker combined to start the strike on this Thursday. (*Reynolds's Weekly Newspaper*)

———◆———

2005: On this day at 8.50 a.m. three bombs were detonated on board three separate London underground trains; the first on a Circle line train travelling between Liverpool Street and Aldgate; the second on another Circle line train travelling between Edgware Road and Paddington; the third on a Piccadilly line train between King's Cross and Russell Square.

Almost an hour later a fourth bomb detonated on a double-decker bus, No. 30, travelling through Tavistock Square. Fifty-two people died and more than 770 people were injured. The four bombers also died. (*Evening Standard*)

JULY 8TH

1732: 'Two labourers, Francis Walford and Thomas Darby, incensed by the comments of a black, William Stanley, returning home to Elmstreet, Gray's Inn', killed him with a shovel. Because they affirmed that he had thrown them a punch before they hit him, they were acquitted of murder on this day. (*Newgate Calendar*)

1907: The City & Guilds College, the Royal School of Mines and the Royal College of Sciences were amalgamated and given a Charter today as the Imperial Collage of Science & Technology, a constituent college of the University of London. It merged with St Mary's Hospital Medical School in 1988 and became a fully independent university in July 2007. (*The Times*)

1932: The Revd Harold Davidson, Rector of Stiffkey, was found guilty by the Church Consistory Court in Westminster, of immoral conduct in respect of Rosie Ellis and Barbara Harris, of improper suggestions to a waitress, of kissing and embracing Miss Harris, of accosting and importuning other waitresses … Politics were the basis of the accusations; he was innocent, but his enemies were more powerful. (*Evening Post*)

JULY 9TH

1822: On this Tuesday London's first nude statue made its appearance in Hyde Park near Apsley House. It was a 5.5m figure of Achilles subscribed for by 'the countrywomen' of England and had a fig leaf added to spare their blushes. At least two attempts have been made to remove it. (*The Times*)

———•◆•———

1860: On this day Florence Nightingale set up the Nightingale Training School at St Thomas's Hospital, and the first Nightingale nurses began work at Liverpool Workhouse Infirmary on 16 May 1865. (*Oxford Dictionary of National Biography*)

———•◆•———

1874: MPs were in full debate when a large tabby cat darted from behind the Speaker's chair, sped over the floor of the house, made a quick spring in the air, leapt across the benches, bounded above heads and disappeared – order was lost in disorder. (Register)

———•◆•———

1877: The first tennis matches were played on this first day of the first ever Wimbledon Lawn Tennis Championships. (*Daily Telegraph*)

JULY 10TH

1212: Only three years after the completion of the first London Bridge to be made of stone, a fire broke out in Southwark and the wind fanned the flames and sent sparks across the bridge, setting fire to it, and trapping the people who had come to help. (City of London Records Office)

1610: The speaker of the House of Commons on this day affirmed that 'Sir E. Herbert put not off his hat to him, but put out his tongue and popped his mouth with his finger in scorn'. (*Palgrave*)

1958: Parkeon installed the first parking meter outside the US Embassy in Grosvenor Square, which was unveiled on this day. It cost *6d* an hour and the fine for non-payment was £2 (about £35 nowadays). (*Daily Telegraph*)

1980: The 105-year-old Exhibition Hall of Alexandra Palace was gutted by a fire that started at 3 p.m. The building had been restored and was to have been unveiled on 11 July. (*Guardian*)

JULY 11TH

1818: A double royal wedding was celebrated on this day at Kew Palace as two brothers, William Duke of Clarence and Edward Duke of Kent married Princess Adelaide of Saxe-Meiningen and Princess Victoria of Saxe-Coburg-Saalfeld respectively.

———◆———

1848: On this day the London & South Western Railway opened Waterloo Bridge station. A spur once led to the adjoining dedicated station of the London Necropolis Co., for funeral trains. (*The Times*)

———◆———

1914: A lady's handbag containing explosives was hung on the back of King Edward's chair in Westminster Abbey and exploded on this day. It blew off part of the chair but the Stone of Scone underneath it was unscathed. (The Times)

———◆———

1936: On this day a De Havilland Rapide piloted by Capt. Cecil Bebb took off from Croydon Airport for Las Palmas where it picked up an obscure army officer and flew him to the mainland to start an insurrection. His name was Franco. (*Guardian*)

———◆———

1976: Brent Cross shopping centre opened. It had eighty-six shops, parking for 5,000 cars, was fully enclosed and air-conditioned, and had a late policy which was novel at this time. (*Evening Standard*)

July 12th

1543: The corpulent and ailing Henry VIII wed Catherine Parr at Hampton Court on this day. She was his last wife.

1845: Pas de Quatre, a ballet choreographed by Jules Perrot and set to music by Cesare Pugni, was first performed at Her Majesty's Theatre on this day. It caused a sensation amongst critics and public alike because it brought together on one stage four of the leading ballerinas of the time. Queen Victoria and Prince Albert attended this third performance. (*The Times*)

1858: Five lives were lost and 300 people were injured when the fireworks of Mr Bennett's in Westminster Road, Lambeth, exploded. Many surrounding houses were destroyed. (*The Times*)

1962: The Marquee Club opened in 1958 as a venue for jazz and skiffle bands. On this day it hosted the first ever performance of the Rolling Stones. (*New York Daily News*)

JULY 13TH

1527: John Dee, future mathematician, astrologer, occultist, imperialist and counsellor to Elizabeth II, was born at Tower ward. (*Oxford Dictionary of National Biography*)

1684: On this day St James's, Piccadilly, was consecrated. The tower, however, was not completed until 1700. (*Victoria County Histories*)

1837: Buckingham Palace, more or less as it is, was completed at a cost of nearly £1 million, and was occupied on this day by Queen Victoria. The Marble Arch was moved to Cumberland Gate, its present position, in 1851.

1911: On this day of the census, the schoolteacher and suffragette Emily Wilding Davidson, was found hiding in the crypt at the House of Parliament, off the St Mary Undercroft chapel. She would later die from injuries sustained when she threw herself under the King's horse at the Derby in 1913 to draw public attention to the public injustice suffered by women. (Census Records)

JULY 14TH

1921: On this Thursday a special correspondent of *The Times* discussed the new fashion of the cocktail, particularly in London, with a distinguished surgeon at the London Hospital. The surgeon opined that, 'one cocktail leads to another, and a series taken a considerable amount of time before a meal may be very harmful indeed'. A visit to a West London establishment resembling the continental 'café' showed that 50 per cent of the clients were women.

———◆———

1989: Fifty-six-year-old Leslie Merry was out shopping in East London on this day when he was hit by a turnip thrown by a passing car. He suffered a punctured lung and a rib was broken in three places. He was hospitalised and got better. When he was released from hospital his condition worsened, and he died of a ruptured spleen on 23 July. Detective Superintendent Graham Howard said the death was being investigated as a murder. (*Daily Express*)

July 15th

1821: Pierce Egan, a journalist, printed the first edition of *Life in London or The Day and Night Scenes of Jerry Hawthorn and his Elegant Friend Corinthian Tom* ... It was an enormous instant success and pirated parts reached America, eventually launching the 'Tom and Jerry' craze. (*Daily Courant*)

1825: The first foundation stone of John Rennie's London Bridge was laid today. His son Sir John Rennie saw it through to completion as his father died before the building work was completed. It was finished in 1831. (The *Times*)

1867: On this day an Act for the preservation of Bunhill Fields Cemetery – last resting place of John Bunyan, George Fox, General Fleetwood and Daniel Defoe, amongst others – as an open space, was passed.

1921: On this Friday the Metropolitan Water Board found it necessary to impose a 'partial service' to the London area, particularly the northern parts as there were already restrictions in the southern and western districts due to the ongoing dry weather that had continued for the previous three weeks. (*The Times*)

July 16th

1546: Anne Askew, who was highly educated in Theology and had been examined for Protestant heresy and racked in the Tower, was on this day carried in a chair because she was so weak, to the stake at Smithfield. (City of London Records Office)

———◆———

1757: A youth of sixteen, James Wales of Fulham, was indicted on this day, having been caught in a compromising situation in the stable of the Peterborough Arms at Parsons Green. He was found making violent love to a horse. Despite protestations he was sentenced to death. (*Newgate Calendar*)

———◆———

1910: On this morning the body of Thomas Weldon Atherton was discovered in the garden of No. 17 Clifton Gardens, Battersea. The elderly stage actor's death was never satisfactorily explained although it was strange that he was found next door to his ex-girlfriend's flat, a much younger woman, despite not living there. (*New York Times*)

July 17th

1841: The first edition of *Punch* appeared today under the joint editorship of Mark Lemon, Henry Mayhew and Stirling Coyne. A gentleman on an omnibus was seen tossing a copy aside and declaring, 'One of these ephemeral things they bring out; won't last a fortnight.' (Mr Watts, RA)

———◆———

1895: The Great Wheel built for the Empire of India Exhibition at Earl's Court was opened to the public on this day and demolished in 1907. (*The Times*)

———◆———

1922: The new London County Council headquarters was formally and partly opened on this day. Ralph Knott, its architect, died aged only twenty-nine. It was his only large commission. (*The Times*)

———◆———

1974: On this day a bomb ripped through the Mortar Room at the Tower of London at 2.30 p.m. The enclosed room was packed with tourists and many people were badly injured. At least two of the victims were children. It was suspected that this was the work of the IRA. (*Evening Standard*)

JULY 18TH

1895: The actor Henry Irving was conferred a knighthood on this day, the first actor to be so recognised. W.E. Gladstone had wanted to offer him one in 1883, but was dissuaded on the grounds that Irving's liaison with Ellen Terry would lead to a row with the Queen over the proposal. (*A Century of Famous Actresses*, Harold Simpson)

———◆———

1921: The works of the Tittanine Co., near Hendon, were destroyed by fire this Monday – *The Times* reported that 'there were many exciting scenes, when drums of varnish were blown into the air and burst with a terrifying noise'.

———◆———

1921: On the same day *The Times* also reported that Nelson Greenaway, a hawker of St Luke's Road, Clapham, was fined £3 at Feltham for colliding into the American Ambassador's car carrying an American General. The American chauffeur had said that the van had skidded because it was going too fast. The defendant's lawyer said that he had made a claim against the embassy but was told that the Ambassador and his suite 'were privileged'.

JULY 19TH

1727: Samuel Hammond of Bishopsgate stabbed his employee to death on this day for calling him a blockhead for using the wrong tools. (*Newgate Calendar*)

1822: Percy Jocelyn, Bishop of Clogher, a habitual 'criminal', was caught in a compromising position with grenadier guardsman John Moverley, in the back room of the White Lion public house, St Albans Place, off the Haymarket. He was eventually deposed for 'crimes of immorality, incontinence, sodomitical practices, habits and propensities.' (*The Times*)

1921: On this Tuesday Arundel Trevanion was fined 40*s* and £3 3*s* costs at Westminster police court for being drunk in charge of a motor car on 8, 9 and 11 July. On each of these days he had been arrested. He admitted all charges. He had had many accidents as an airman and suffered from shell shock. (*The Times*)

July 20th

1841: The Fenchurch Street railway station, the first to be built inside the City, was opened on this day. It was the location of the first railway bookstall in the City, operated by William Marshall. (*Standard*)

———•◆•———

1885: This evening at Anderton's Hotel on Fleet Street, members of the Football Association met to listen to and accept a report that stipulated that a footballer who received any remuneration or payment of any expenses would have to be termed as a professional. (FA)

———•◆•———

1921: Sir Edward Elgar opened the new premises of the Gramophone Co. Ltd at No. 363-7 Oxford Street this Wednesday, twenty five years after the first gramophone was made in England as a scientific toy. (*The Times*)

———•◆•———

1982: The Provisional IRA detonated two bombs in Hyde Park and Regent's Park on this day. The bombs killed eight soldiers, wounded forty-seven people and led to the death of seven horses. (*Evening Standard*)

July 21st

1858: The Minutes of the Royal Zoological Society showed that letters this day were received from Messrs Mivart & Ackerley respecting the gatekeeper's refusal to admit certain persons to whom they had given admissions to the gardens on the grounds that they had been badly dressed.

———◆———

1921: The inquest on the death of Sir Alfred Newton, chairman of Harrods Ltd, was resumed this Thursday after being adjourned twice. In earlier evidence an analyst had found sufficient strychnine in a medicine bottle to kill a considerable number of people. The jury eventually returned a verdict of death caused by strychnine poisoning, helped by syncope. (*The Times*)

———◆———

2005: On this Thursday, a second series of four explosions took place on the London Underground and a London bus. The detonators of all the bombs exploded, but not the explosives. There were no casualties. The single injury reported was later revealed to be the result of an asthma attack. All the bombers escaped but were later arrested. (*Daily Mail*)

JULY 22ND

1965: Three Rolling Stones, Mick Jagger, Keith Richards and Bill Wyman, were found guilty on this day in East Ham Magistrate's Court of insulting behaviour after urinating on the wall of a London petrol station when the owner refused to let them used the toilet. They were each fined £5. (*East Ham Recorder*)

———◆———

1972: On this day Chi Chi, the London Zoo's giant panda, died after nearly fourteen years in the zoo. (Zoological Society, annual report, 1972)

———◆———

2005: On this day the police had a block of flats in Tulse Hill under surveillance because they believed one of the failed 21 July bombers lived there. They mistook the young Brazilian Jean Charles de Menezes as him, followed him to Stockwell station and shot him dead. (*Daily Mail*)

July 23rd

1690: Richard Gibson, aged seventy-five, court painter and court dwarf to Charles I, died on this day. His wife, Anne Shepherd, also a dwarf, died ten years later. She had been court dwarf to Queen Henrietta Maria. (*Chamber's Book of Days*)

———◆———

1863: Alexandra Park, named as a tribute to the Princess of Wales, was opened to the public on this Thursday with a flower show, fruit show and other kindred entertainments. It had been opened pro-forma the previous Monday, and *The Times* were wont to describe it as the Bois de Boulogne of Holloway or Highgate.

———◆———

1986: On this Wednesday Prince Andrew wed Sarah Ferguson at Westminster Abbey and 2,000 people attended. They drove back to Buckingham Palace in the open-topped 1902 State Landau. (*The Times*)

———◆———

2011: On this day the singer Amy Winehouse was found dead in her Camden apartment. (*Daily Mail*)

JULY 24TH

1721: The Boarding House on Marylebone Fields on this day gave a show of a panther fighting twelve dogs for a prize of £300, one dog at a time. The entry tickets cost *2s 6d* or *2s*. (*Morning Chronicle*)

—◆—

1969: After four years in a Soviet jail for subversive anti-Soviet activity in the Soviet Union, Gerald Brooke, aged thirty-one, returned to London on this day. He had been swapped with Mr and Mrs Kroger, a couple involved in the Portland spy case. (*The Times*)

—◆—

1987: Jeffery Archer was on this day awarded record libel damages of £500,000 and costs from the *Star* newspaper for accusing him of paying a prostitute, Monica Coghlan, for sex. The former deputy chairman of the Conservative party told the jury he was a fool for paying £2,000 to her, but that he was not a liar when he denied having slept with her. (*Guardian*)

—◆—

1990: On this early Monday morning the bodies of two murdered women, Patricia Morrison and Miss Forsyth, were found sprawled in Miss Morrison's beige Toyota Corolla in Spears Road, Hornsey. Both had been strangled. (*Daily Mail*)

JULY 25TH

1837: William Cooke, at Camden Town, and Charles Wheatstone, professor of Experimental Physics at King's College, at Euston, two stations nineteen miles apart, exchanged messages on their five-needle telegraph, showing the commercial viability of this method of communication. (*Oxford Dictionary of National Biography*)

———◆———

1865: Dr James Barry, former Inspector General of Hospitals, died on this day aged about sixty-six, near Cavendish Square. The woman who laid out the corpse affirmed that Dr Barry was a woman and had had a child. If this was the case, then technically Barry was not only the youngest, but the first woman to graduate in medicine. (*Oxford Dictionary of National Biography*)

———◆———

1914: W.G. Grace battled for the last time for Eltham Cricket Club at Grove Park, aged sixty-six. He contributed an undefeated 69 to a total of 155-6 declared. He was also the first English captain to surrender the urn when England lost in 1891/2. (*Wisden's*)

JULY 26TH

1818: A clown called Usher drove a carriage pulled by four tom-cats along the Waterloo Road on this day as a publicity stunt for the new theatre, the Royal Coburg Theatre, later named the Old Vic. (*The Times*)

1849: 'Between the first bursting of the drains on this day and that on the 2nd of August, there have been three cases of cholera, one of which has already terminated fatally, and a case of choleric diarrhoea. On the morning after the second storm three or four persons were attacked, and the attacks continued numerous for three or four days.' (John Snow's Account of Cholera on Albion Terrace, Wandsworth Road – *Medical Gazette*)

1994: A car, packed with 20-30lb of explosives, blew up outside the Israeli embassy at about midday on this day. It blew up moments after the driver left it. (*Evening Standard*)

JULY 27TH

1695: On this day the Bank of England received its Royal Charter. Sir John Houblon, a Huguenot, was its first director.

———•—•———

1732: On this day a great cricket match was played at Kew. Frederick Prince of Wales attended. (*Whitehall Evening Post*)

———•—•———

1781: François Henri de La Motte, a French officer, was publicly hanged at Tyburn, watched by 80,000. His heart was burned. He had been found guilty of sending naval intelligence to France. (*Newgate Calendar*)

———•—•———

1888: Today was the inauguration of the Union of Women Matchmakers. By the end of the year the Union changed its name and rules to the Matchmakers Union, open to men and women.

———•—•———

1990: Marcel Marceau, the mime artist, proved he was a monologue artist of the first order at a press conference at the Savoy on this day. He spoke for twenty-five minutes then answered twenty-five minutes of questions – possibly his last one-man show in London. (*The Times*)

JULY 28TH

1722: In *Saturday's Post* it was proposed on this day that street oil lamps be installed and lit every night of the year, as a way of fighting street robberies on 'nights that are as dark as in the midst of Winter'.

———◆———

1761: Walking home this evening Giles Cooper discovered William Bailey and Robert Stimpson, in a passage near Ball Alley, Lombard Street, with both their breeches down – their pose left little to the imagination. (*Proceedings of the Old Bailey*)

———◆———

1866: Beatrix Potter was born at No. 2 Bolton Gardens, Kensington, close to Brompton Cemetery. (Registers of Births, Marriages and Deaths)

———◆———

1906: The Tooting Lido, England's largest public swimming pool at 50m long, opened on this day as the Tooting Bathing Lake. (*Borough News*)

———◆———

1931: Flt-Lt Reginald Goddard, managing director of a Battersea-based slate and slab firm, opened Chessington Zoo to show the public his animal collection. (*The Times*)

JULY 29TH

1829: The first thousand Metropolitan Policemen dressed in blue tailcoats, top hats, truncheons, handcuffs and a rattle started to patrol the streets of London. (Metropolitan Police Archives)

—————•·•—————

1859: The last performance at Vauxhall Gardens took place on this day. The ground was sold for redevelopment. (*The Times*)

—————•·•—————

1948: The summer Olympics opened on this day in London after twelve years' hiatus because of the war. A record fifty-nine nations were represented in nineteen disciplines. (*Daily Telegraph*)

—————•·•—————

1981: On this day 600,000 people filled the London streets to catch a glimpse of Prince Charles and Lady Diana Spencer on their wedding day – they married in St Paul's. This had an estimated global audience of 750 million, which made it the most popular programme ever broadcast. (*The Times*)

—————•·•—————

1990: Police arrested a Syrian gunman, Ham el Rayes, who had threatened to kill clubbers, after a ten-hour siege of Tokyo Jo club in Clarges Street. Some of his relatives were being held hostage in the Lebanon. (*The Times*)

July 30th

1746: On this Wednesday nine Roman Catholic Jacobite members of the Manchester Regiment were hanged, drawn and quartered on Kennington Common. (*Newgate Calendar*)

1900: The Central Line of the London underground opened on this day with a service between Shepherd's Bush and Bank stations. The line was extremely popular and had a flat fare of 2*d* – prompting the papers to call it the 'Two Penny Tube'. (London Transport Museum)

1966: A crowd of 93,000, including the Queen and Prince Philip, watched England win football's World Cup over West Germany at Wembley Stadium. (*Daily Mail*)

1991: The Italian tenor Luciano Pavarotti celebrated thirty years in opera by singing to 100,000 fans in the pouring rain in Hyde Park. It was the largest concert in Hyde Park since the Rolling Stones performed there in 1969. (*Daily Mail*)

July 31st

1888: At Marylebone, Walter Hamilton Goodfellow, described as a gentleman living at Ladbroke Gardens, Kensington, was charged on remand with stealing a bell bird, valued at £10, the property of the Zoological Society. He was fined £5 and ordered to pay the value of the bird. (*The Times*)

1895: At Baldwyn's Park, Sydenham, on this day, Mr Hyram Maxim's gargantuan flying machine with a 105ft wingspan, weighing more than 7,000lb and powered by steam engines, lifted off a 1,800ft test track and flew 600ft. (*New York Times*)

1950: The first self-service Sainsbury's store opened in Croydon. It wasn't, however, immediately popular. One local magazine even said that it 'was the easiest way in the world of spending too much money' in a period of post-war austerity. (*Croydon Advertiser*)

August 1st

1715: The first Doggett's Coat and Badge race, the oldest rowing contest in the world, took place on the Thames, starting at London Bridge and ending in Chelsea.

———•◆•———

1820: The Regent's Canal, starting at Paddington, meandering through Maida Vale, Regent's Park, Islington, Hoxton, Hackney, Mile End to Limehouse, where it joins the Thames, was opened on this day. (*The Times*)

———•◆•———

1831: John Rennie's New London Bridge was officially opened. King William IV and Queen Adelaide attended a banquet in a pavilion erected on the bridge. (*The Times*)

———•◆•———

1861: *The Times* published the first ever weather forecast today for the general public. Admiral Robert Fitzroy was its inceptor. He was reprimanded, despite the 'forecast' being accurate, as his superiors did not believe his predictions were accurate.

———•◆•———

1965: A brand new group called the Steam Packet was the supporting group for the Rolling Stones at the London Palladium. It featured vocals by one Rod Stewart. (*Illustrated Encyclopaedia of Music*)

AUGUST 2ND

1833: Vauxhall Gardens, the famous entertainment gardens, had their most successful day when 133,278 people visited and the receipts were £29,590. (*The Gentleman's Magazine*)

1870: On this day the Tower subway, a tunnel running between Tower Hill and Vine Lane on the South Bank, was opened. Originally intended for 'cable' cars, it was turned into a pedestrian walkway. (Civil Engineering Heritage)

1875: The first roller-skating rink, the Belgravia Roller Skating Rink, opened. (*Victoria County History*)

1897: Jeremy Morris, aged ten, bathing in the Grand Junction Canal, sacrificed his life to help his sinking companion. (Memorial to Heroic Self Sacrifice – Postman's Park)

1921: On this Tuesday several residents of North London boroughs Hackney and Upper Clapton were summoned to the North London Police court. They were fined for illegally using a hose for watering their gardens as they had not paid their garden rate – the dry period continues. (*The Times*)

AUGUST 3RD

1916: On this day at 9 a.m. Roger David Casement was hanged at Pentonville Prison. He had been a much admired high-ranking Anglo–Irish civil servant whose administrative and humanitarian skills were widely admired. Disillusioned with Britain's Imperialist policy, he sought Germany's help in gaining freedom for Ireland, and was caught. He was accused of high treason, sabotage and espionage, and his honours were revoked. One of his many admirers, Mrs Huth Jackson, sent her daughter, Konradin, daily to his cell with a clean shirt. (*The Times*)

1926: The first traffic lights in London were erected at the junction of Piccadilly and St James Street on this day. They were operated manually by policemen in a signal box. (*Illustrated London News*)

1955: The English language version of the play *Waiting for Godot* by Samuel Becket was first performed at the Arts Theatre. On hearing the now famous line 'nothing happens, nobody comes, nobody goes, it's awful', a wag shouted 'hear, hear'. (*Samuel Beckett – A Biography*, Deirdre Bair)

AUGUST 4TH

1586: Back from plundering the Spanish in the New World, Sir Francis Drake was feted in the Middle Temple on this day. (City of London Records Office)

1914: The crowd were enjoying an open-air concert given by a German band at the Earl's Court Exhibition when the bandmaster stopped the music and announced, 'Ladies and Gentlemen, war has been declared'. The musicians filed out silently. (*The Times*)

1921: On this Thursday the London County Council tramway extension along Wandsworth High Street and East Hill was opened. (London Transport Museum)

2000: Celebrations took place in London and all over the country to celebrate the 100th birthday of HM Elizabeth, the Queen Mother. She died in 2002. (*The Times*)

2011: Mark Duggan, a mixed-race gang member, was shot in in Tottenham on this day. The police were accused. (*Daily Telegraph*)

August 5th

1901: The Mowhawk Hall, in Islington, a theatre with stalls and balcony forming part of the Agricultural Hall, showed its first film on 3 August 3 1900, and was dedicated to film on this day. It became a bingo hall in the 1960s. (*Daily Mail*)

————•◆•————

1911: The Radium Picture Playhouse opened as a conversion form a gymnasium in No. 65 Drayton Gardens, Lower Chelsea, on this day. It later became the Paris Pullman. (*Victoria County Histories*)

————•◆•————

1955: The *Guardian* critic said of *Waiting for Godot* by Samuel Beckett, that 'the play bored some people acutely. Others found it a witty and poetic conundrum'.

————•◆•————

1965: The *Guardian* reported on this day that an electronic push-button system of instant voting, which would cut the time taken up by divisions in the Commons by ten minutes, was recommended in a report by the unofficial Parliamentary Reform group.

August 6th

1844: The birth of Queen Victoria's second son. Alfred Ernest, at Windsor Castle, was transmitted to the offices of *The Times* in central London within forty minutes on this day. *The Times* reported this story as being 'in debt to the extraordinary power of the electromagnetic telegraph'.

1889: The Savoy Hotel, just off the Strand, built by Richard D'Oyly Carte, was opened. The first luxury hotel in Britain, it was the first to have electric lifts and lights. Its first manager was César Ritz and its chef was August Escoffier. It is the only street in London where cars drive on the right. (*The Times*)

1966: Muhammad Ali beat Brian London at a boxing match at the Exhibition Hall, Earl's Court on this day. (*Daily Telegraph*)

2011: After a memorial march for the death of Mark Duggan, rioting broke out in Tottenham and shops were looted and set alight. (*Daily Telegraph*)

AUGUST 7TH

1746: The Jacobite captain, James Dawson, was hanged, drawn and quartered on Kennington Common today. His fiancée died seconds after watching the execution. (*Whitehall Evening Post*)

———•◆•———

1821: On this day the ill-starred Caroline of Brunswick expired, stricken down, as was generally alleged, by vexation at being refused admission to Westminster Abbey in the previous month when she desired to participate in the coronation ceremonies of her consort George IV. The immediate cause, however, was an illness by which she was suddenly attacked at Drury Lane Theatre, and which ran its course in the space of a few days. (*Chamber's Book of Days*)

———•◆•———

2011: Rioting and looting spread across London and beyond. Brixton, Enfield, Islington, Wood Green and Oxford Circus were scenes of the rioting – many looters didn't even bother to mask themselves. (*Daily Mail*)

AUGUST 8TH

1902: The British Academy received its Royal Charter from King Edward VII on the eve of his coronation. (Register)

————◆•————

1988: The Duke and Duchess of York today announced the birth of their first child, a daughter, later called Beatrice Elizabeth Mary, at the Portland Hospital. (*The Times*)

————◆•————

2011: The riots continued London-wide: Battersea, Brixton, Bromley, Camden, Chingford Mount, Croydon, Ealing, East Ham, Hackney, Harrow, Lewisham, Peckham, Waltham Forest and Woolwich shops were looted. Waterstone's on St John's Road, Battersea, was spared. At least 1,000 were arrested in London. There were two deaths and this was the first use of mobile phones to organise looting and rioting activities – and the first time mobile logs were used to make arrests. (*Evening Standard*)

AUGUST 9TH

1611: Maudlin Tichon, a sharp-tongued woman of the parish of St Martin-in-the-Fields, was towed across the Thames at the tail of a boat for her wicked tongue. (City of London Records Office)

———◆———

1901: The fifty-nine-year-old Albert Edward was crowned Edward VII at Westminster Abbey. The coronation had been scheduled for 26 June, but he developed appendicitis just two days before. Thanks to the surgical skills of Frederick Treves, he recovered quickly. (*The Times*)

———◆———

1963: *Ready Steady Go!* premiered at a small studio in Kingsway. Its first guests were Pat Boone, Billy Fury, Burl Ives and Brian Poole, as well as the Tremeloes. (BBC)

———◆———

1980: Ten original Gerald Scarfe drawings for Pink Floyd's album 'The Wall' were stolen from the foyer of Earl's Court where they were being exhibited. (*Daily Mail*)

AUGUST 10TH

1660: Samuel Pepys recorded that on this day he went with Mr Moor and Creed to Hyde Park, by coach, and saw a fine foot-race three times round the park.

———◆———

1675: One of Wren's many projects, apart from building fifty churches, two theatres and Temple Bar, was also the designing of Flamsteed House, home of the first Greenwich Observatory. King Charles II, a keen astronomer, laid the first stone on this day. (City of London Records Office)

———◆———

1779: John By was baptised at St Mary's Lambeth today. He became a British military engineer, and as such was sent to supervise the building of the Rideau Canal in Canada. He constructed a town in the Ottawa River valley to house the canal workers and in so doing created what was to become Canada's capital city. (*Oxford Dictionary of National Biography*)

———◆———

1848: A.W.N. Pugin, the architect who designed St George's Roman Catholic cathedral in Southwark, was the first person to be married there, to his third wife Jane. (Parish Registers)

AUGUST 11TH

1668: Samuel Pepys recorded that, 'this afternoon, my wife, Mercer and Deb went with Pelling to see the Gypsies at Lambeth and have their fortunes told, but what they did, I did not enquire.'

———◆———

1897: Enid Blyton was born on this day at No. 354 Lordship Lane, East Dulwich, to Thomas Carey Blyton and Theresa Harrison. (Registers)

———◆———

1982: Ronnie and Reggie Kray were allowed out of prison on this day for their mother's funeral service in the East End, but they were not allowed to attend her burial. (*Daily Mail*)

———◆———

2003: Lord Hutton's inquiry into the death of Dr David Kelly, the MOD expert on biological warfare found dead shortly after he had made assertions on the credibility of Mr Blair's reasons for going to war in Iraq, started on this day. It would deliver its contentious verdict in 2004, absolving the government of any wrongdoing. (*Guardian*)

AUGUST 12TH

1707: From this day there was an epidemic of flies in London, for at least four days. Henry Chamberlain wrote that 'the epidemic was so prodigious that the people's feet made as full an impression on them as upon thick snow'.

───◆───

1797: Teresa Cornelys, the opera singer and grande dame of the London 'Haut Ton', whose parties and assemblies had electrified high society, died at an advanced age in the hospital room of the Fleet, which the humanity of the warden bestowed on her. (*Oxford Dictionary of National Biography*)

───◆───

1822: Although his wife succeeded in removing all razors and his doctor was constantly in attendance, Viscount Castlereagh managed to find a penknife and committed suicide by cutting his own throat in his London home. (*Oxford Dictionary of National Biography*)

───◆───

2003: Andrew Gilligan, the journalist at the centre of the controversy surrounding the death of weapons expert Dr David Kelly, admitted today that his language 'wasn't perfect' when he reported the government had 'sexed up' its weapons dossier on Iraq. (*Guardian*)

AUGUST 13TH

1899: Alfred Joseph Hitchcock was born on this day to a greengrocer and poulterer at Leytonstone. It was whilst working at Henley's, a cable company, that he developed a creative talent, producing articles and becoming intrigued by photography and the moving image. He started directing films in 1922 and his first major success, *The Lodger, a Story of the London Fog*, established his reputation. His tenth film, 'Blackmail', is widely considered to be the first British 'talkie'. (*Oxford Dictionary of National Biography*)

———◆———

1921: On this Saturday evening the matron of Dr Barnardo's Home for Boys at No. 49 High Street, Clapham, was attacked by two men at her front door at 10 p.m., when they had established that her husband, the superintendent, wasn't at home. They struck her and gagged her, cut her hair and ransacked the office. She passed out, but once she awoke she asked a student to telephone the police. (*Daily Mail*)

AUGUST 14TH

1666: '… And after Dinner with my wife and Mercer to the Bear Garden … and saw some good sport of the bull's tossing of the clogs – one into the very boxes. But it is a very rude and nasty pleasure.' (Pepys)

***

1888: An audio recording of the composer Arthur Sullivan's *The Lost Chord*, one of the first recordings of music ever made, was played during a press conference introducing Thomas Edison's phonograph cylinder in London. (*The Times*)

***

1948: The closing ceremony of the 'Austerity' 14th Olympic Games, hosted by the United Kingdom, was held at the Empire Stadium, Wembley. (*The Times*)

***

2011: The London–Surrey Classic Cycle race took place on this Sunday, starting at Pall Mall and covering fifty miles through Surrey – the event that was a precursor to the 2012 Olympic Games. (*Daily Telegraph*)

AUGUST 15TH

1921: A conference was held at the Oval on this day to consider the questions relating to Imperial cricket. One of Australia's proposals was to increase the overs from 6-8 balls – this was strongly opposed. (*The Times*)

1921: On the same day a fifteen-year-old boy entered a branch of the London County, Westminster & Parr's Bank on Streatham High Road and asked for a 5½ per cent Treasury bond on behalf of a local known resident. When the clerk turned his back the boy seized a bundle of £1,000 in Treasury notes and disappeared. (*The Times*)

1921: On the same day the first baby in arms to travel on the Continental Airways left London Croydon Airstation for Paris. The 5½-month-old Swiss, Frieda Inglin, slept the whole way.

1941: Josef Jakobs, a German spy, was the last person to be executed in the Tower of London by firing squad. Because he had a broken ankle he was shot sitting down. (*Daily Mail*)

AUGUST 16TH

1749: The *Daily Advertiser* reported that 'a resurrection had begun a commotion in Shoreditch Parish. Yesterday it was said that Topham, the strongman had, the night before, with the assistance of some surgeons, got the better of his grave, though some eight feet of earth had been laid on him'.

———◆———

1851: The Mansion House court was densely packed on this Saturday because of the Lord Mayor's inquiry into the death of a man named Cogan, alias John Bell, whose death was alleged to have been caused by violence on the part of an officer of the City Police Force named John Cole. (*Observer*)

———◆———

1897: The Tate Gallery was opened. It was, along with a collection of sixty-seven Victorian paintings, a gift from the sugar magnate Sir Henry Tate. (*The Times*)

———◆———

2008: As the night drew in on this Monday and the Notting Hill Festival drew to a close, forty young men fought a running battle with the police in West London – it lasted more than two hours. (*Independent*)

AUGUST 17TH

1817: Waterloo Bridge, then known as the 'Strand Bridge', was opened on this day – it was pulled down in 1936. (*The Times*)

1850: A tailor, Henry Derby, was charged on this Saturday before Alderman Gibbs at the Mansion House Court, with having acted in an indecent manner towards two girls aged between twelve and fourteen. The prisoner was stated to have been a long time pursuing these two poor children, but there were such discrepancies in the evidence that he had to be discharged. (*Observer*)

1896: The horseless carriage had arrived in Britain. Three imported Roger-Benz vehicles were being exhibited at the Dolphin Terrace, Crystal Palace. Arthur Edsall, the driver of one, drove at bewildering speed, 4mph, and erratically knocked down and fatally injured Bridget Driscoll who was attending a Catholic League of the Cross fête with her sixteen-year-old daughter. She was the country's first fatal car accident victim. (*Norwood News*)

AUGUST 18TH

1274: King Edward I received an enthusiastic welcome in London on his arrival, a full two years after his accession. (City of London Records Office)

1667: Samuel Pepys recorded in his diary that he made a pass at a young woman in the congregation at St Dunstan-in-the-West, in Fleet Street.

1749: Two soldiers found guilty of desertion, detained in the Savoy Prison, were marched up Birdcage Walk and then led to the stone on the north side of Hyde Park. They prayed for fifteen minutes in the hope of a reprieve, but none came. Caps were put over their eyes; a firing team of six and a reserve of six carried out the execution. (*Penny London Post*)

1877: On this Saturday John Coleman and Charles Thompson were charged with loitering with intent to pick pockets. They had been following two ladies from Fleet Street to Cheapside. (*Observer*)

August 19th

1886: Joseph Provin, Adrien Favier and Rosa Jourdain, all of French nationality and claiming to be from Avignon, were charged with having in their possession a quantity of gold, diamonds and other jewellery, all stolen from Nimes, which they tried to sell on this day to Mr George Henry Allen of Soho Square in Mr Percy Edwards' shop in Piccadilly. (*Observer*)

———————

1897: The first Mulliner-bodied Bersey taxis (electric cars) went into service on this day in London. They were the first self-propelled taxis and were nicknamed Hummingbirds because of their low engine noise. (London Transport Museum)

———————

1999: Jeff Smith of Muswell Hill, a Freeman of the City of London, drove two sheep, Clover and Little Man, across Tower Bridge, claiming he was exercising an ancient permission granted to Freemen, and to make a point on the perceived erosion of the rights of older citizens. (*The Times*)

AUGUST 20TH

1811: Parson's Green Fair was ordered to be prevented on this day by the Bishop of London, but having on enquiry learnt that the fair was remarkable for its good old English gaiety and was countenanced by all the good families of the neighbourhood, the Bishop gave notice that he should not interfere. (*Jackson's Oxford Journal*)

———◆———

1853: On this Saturday, Amelia Hilliard, a lady thief, residing at No. 2 Great Quebec Street, was charged at Marylebone Court with stealing a bottle of brandy from the bar of the Lincoln Hotel, South Street, Manchester Square. The ladylike, well-dressed woman wept bitterly, but was committed to trial. (*Observer*)

———◆———

1929: The BBC made the first transmission using the thirty-line mechanically scanned television system, developed by John Logie Baird.

———◆———

1989: The pleasure boat *Marchioness* sank after being run down by the dredger *Bowbelle* near Cannon Street Railway Bridge. Fifty-one people drowned. (*Evening Standard*)

AUGUST 21ST

1806: The *Morning Post* advertised on this day the sale of 'a good second-hand, sociable body, with head and kneeboot, sound and will be dispos'd of at reasonable price, the owner having no further use of it'.

1906: George Gamble of Commercial Street, a painter's labourer with Trollope & Colls, went to a prostitute he knew in Brick Lane. PC Ashford told him to move on and himself asked the prostitute for her services for free. She refused and went after Mr Gamble. PC Ashford beat Gamble up so badly that he was in the London Hospital for three months with a ruptured urethra. His was one of the few complaints that the police upheld! (*The Times*)

1936: Senate House, the University of London's administrative building, the tallest building in the country at the time, was officially opened on this day. (*The Times*)

1996: The new Globe Theatre was opened on this day with a production of *The Two Gentlemen of Verona*.

AUGUST 22ND

1800: Camberwell Fair 'commenced with no less than eight theatres, besides Punch, Beasts, etc., "Old Drury" is erected on the green and Pizarro strutted his hour upon the stage some dozen times'. (*Jackson's Oxford Journal*)

———◆———

1809: A duel took place on this day in a field between Highgate and Hampstead Heath between two Hibernians, not by pugilism, but with cudgels, their national weapons. They fought for an hour and five minutes with the greater desperation until O'Reilly fell to the ground covered in contusions. (*London Gazette*)

———◆———

1854: On one day magistrates spent three hours dealing with cases arising from the fair at Camberwell, including numerous children, as young as nine or ten, who were charged with pickpocketing. (*The Times*)

———◆———

1906: Marguerite Radclyffe Hall, better known as 'John', poet, writer and very public lesbian, met Mabel Veronica Batten at a lunch at the Savoy Hotel. 'John' and 'Ladye' lived together in 1915 when 'John' met her other love, Una, Lady Troubridge.

AUGUST 23RD

1305: William Wallace, the Scots war leader and resistance fighter against Edward I, was brought to London and on this day tried at Westminster Hall, charged with treason and murder. He was dragged to Smithfield and hanged, drawn and quartered there – making him a martyr. (City of London Records Office)

1792: Henry Walton Smith died on this day. Shortly before his death he had purchased a 'Newswalk' business based on premises in Little Grosvenor Street, Mayfair. This was the foundation of WH Smith & Sons.

1796: On this day, the month of his seventeenth birthday, Robert Barclay, the future celebrated pedestrian, took on his first sporting wager to walk from his school in Brixton, Loughborough House, six miles to Croydon, inside an hour. He completed it successfully.

2010: On this Monday evening the police entered the second-floor Pimlico flat of thirty-one-year-old Gareth Williams, a GCHQ operative on secondment to MI6. He had been missing for six weeks. They found his badly decomposed body locked in a holdall in his bath. (*Guardian*)

AUGUST 24TH

1770: Loneliness, hunger and an abundance of self-pity made Thomas Chatterton take a dose of arsenic, bought to poison the rats that infested the garret he lived in, and where he died. Lauded by Johnson as a literary genius, praised by Coleridge, Shelley and Byron for his contributions to their understanding of mediaeval poetry, Chatterton was a fraud and liar. His original work was undistinguished, but his forgery of 'mediaeval' manuscripts was without parallel. (*Oxford Dictionary of National Biography*)

———•◆•———

1795: Patent 2061 was granted on this day to the Revd Samuel Henshall, later vicar of St Mary-le-Bow, designer of the first corkscrew with a button on top to break any residual bond between cork and bottle-top. The engineer was Matthew Boulton. (Patent Office)

———•◆•———

1940: On this night German bombers lost their way over blacked-out Britain and accidentally dropped their bombs on London instead of the intended target, the oil refinery at Thameshaven.

AUGUST 25TH

1619: On this day King James I and his favourite, George Villiers, Duke of Buckingham, visited and stayed the night at the Chicken House on Hampstead High Street. (City of London Records Office)

1825: On this Thursday the editor of the *Morning Post* directed the reader's attention to the first annual report of the meritorious Society of London, which had been instituted for the Prevention of Cruelty to Animals. It would be read with great interest by everyone who acknowledged the importance of the institution and the moral duty which is its object to enforce.

1840: The conductor of one of Chancellor's Chelsea omnibuses found a pocket book containing £150 and cheques under one of the seats. Several notes in the pocket book led him to Mr Kempis on New Road. The gentleman was so overcome by the conductor's honesty that he gave him £60. (*Jackson's Oxford Journal*)

AUGUST 26TH

1791: Jeanne de St Remy de Valois, Comtesse de la Motte, was buried in the churchyard of St Mary's, Lambeth. She had died on the 23rd, jumping from a window whilst fleeing her creditors. She was the infamous instigator of 'Le Collier de la Reine' (the Queen's Necklace) incident that set the flames of the French Revolution. (*Courier*)

1899: Just a month after the New Cross Empire Theatre opened under Mr Stoll's management, the ERA newspaper lauded the immense success of Mr Arthur Lloyd with *Son and Daughter*.

1921: The *Quest*, the ship that would carry Sir Ernest Shackleton and his crew to the Antarctic, was being filled out in St Katherine's Dock. (*The Times*)

1974: Two of the cars on the big dipper at Battersea funfair jammed on this evening, 40ft above ground. After nearly two hours twenty-four people, most of them children, were evacuated by firemen. (*Guardian*)

AUGUST 27TH

1921: Adelaide Louise Jones of Chelsea, aged sixty, was remanded on this day at Bow Street Police Court for maliciously injuring the original will of the late William Thomas. She had asked permission to read the will at Somerset House and returned it torn, saying that she had done it as it was a forgery and that there was no other course open to her. (*The Times*)

1967: Brian Epstein, the Beatles' manager, was found dead at his Belgravia home. A post-mortem examination showed that he had died of an overdose of sleeping pills. It was officially ruled as accidental, although it has been speculated that it was suicide. (*The Times*)

1990: Ernest Saunders, Gerald Ronson, Sir Jack Lyons and Anthony Parnes were convicted on this day at Southwark Crown Court. They were charged due to their involvement in a conspiracy to drive up the prices of shares in Guinness during a 1986 takeover battle for the drinks company, Distillers. Lyons was stripped of his knighthood, and Saunders, Ronson and Parnes were sentenced to periods in prison ranging from twelve months to five years. (*Daily Mail*)

AUGUST 28TH

1577: On this day the first stone was laid for the foundations of Nonesuch House on London Bridge. Built entirely of wood above foundation level, it was held together by pre-formed pegs and was still standing when the houses on the bridge were being demolished in 1757!

1985: Reinhard and Sonja Schulze appeared before Horseferry Road Magistrates Court accused of possessing documents detrimental to the public interest, under the Official Secrets Act. (*Daily Telegraph*)

1996: On this day Buckingham Palace issued a press release regarding the decree absolute of the divorce between the Prince and Princess of Wales. The press release stated that Diana had lost the style of Her Royal Highness and instead was styled Diana, Princess of Wales. (*The Diana Chronicles*, Tina Brown)

2003: A blackout in south-east England put 500,000 people in the dark and shut down half the railways in London. It was the biggest blackout in England since 1987, though it only lasted thirty-four minutes. (*Evening Standard*)

August 29th

1891: Joe Deakin, a Walsall anarchist, got chatting to Auguste Coulon in the Anarchic Bar. They discussed obtaining bombs for use in Tsarist Russia. It turned out Coulon was a police spy. Walsall was later arrested. (*The Slow Burning Fuse*, John Quail)

1958: A gang of Teddy Boys attacked a white woman who was married to a black man. The police managed to take her home, but a mob of about 400 later attacked Bromley Road, causing damage to houses of the Afro-Caribbean community. The riots swelled to an angry mob of 1,000, but petered out by 5 September. (*The Times*)

1975: A former army officer, Roger Goad, an explosives officer with the London Metropolitan Police, was called to look at a suspicious package on Kensington Church Street, W11. He attempted to defuse the bomb, but it exploded, killing him instantly. The bomb had been placed by the IRA unit that was eventually captured at the Balcombe Street Siege. (*The Times*)

AUGUST 30TH

1572: On this day Elizabeth I issued a ban on football in the streets, 'no foteball player be used or suffered within the City of London and the liberties thereof upon pain of imprisonment', to no effect!

1889: Oscar Wilde and Arthur Conan Doyle dined at the Langham Hotel with the publishers of *Lippincott's Monthly Magazine*. This meeting led to *The Sign of Four* and *The Picture of Dorian Gray*. (Plaque)

1976: When the police tried to arrest a pickpocket at the Notting Hill Carnival, other youths went to help him, resulting in a riot in which sixty-six people were arrested. Sixty carnival-goers needed hospital treatment, as did more than 100 police officers. (*Guardian*)

2003: Bermondsey's Twin Parks Festival took place on this sunny Saturday afternoon in Leathermarket Gardens and Tabard Gardens. The event was organised by the West Bermondsey Community Forum, a 'neighbourhood Renewal Initiative'. (*SE1 Magazine*)

AUGUST 31ST

1723: The *London Journal* commented that 'scarce a week passes, but we have a Boxing Match at the Bear Garden between women'.

———◆———

1724: Jonathan Wild, thief and thief-taker, successfully managed to have the diminutive Jack 'Gentleman Jack' Sheppard arrested and imprisoned in Newgate, pending his execution for theft. On this very day when Sheppard's death warrant arrived, he loosened a bar in his cell window and, disguised as a woman, escaped the prison. (*Newgate Calendar*)

———◆———

1854: A severe outbreak of cholera occurred at Broad Street, now Broadwick Street, in Soho. By the end of the outbreak 616 people died. Dr John Snow was convinced, unlike his peers, that the cause was contaminated water. It was cholera. (John Snow Society)

———◆———

1891: Sally the chimpanzee died at the Zoological Gardens. The *Daily News* commented that her intelligence was the subject of comment amongst men of science, of sages and philosophers. Poor Sally's death had been previously reported, but it actually took place on this Friday.

SEPTEMBER 1ST

1767: A two-year-old child, Elizabeth Ayres, was run over by James Woodman in his cart on King Edward's Street. The wheel passed over her jaw, killing her instantly. His punishment was to be burnt on the hands and released. (Old Bailey Archives)

1921: Writs were on this day issued to members of the Poplar Council for failure to levy the local rates. The reason given by the Borough Councillors for their refusal to levy these local rates was that the people of Poplar were unable to pay the high rates demanded. (*The Times*)

1951: *The Grocer* reported that '1,500 South London housewives performed their own opening ceremony of the new self-service shop, The Premier Store, on Streatham High Street today'. This was arguably the first supermarket in Britain.

1968: The Walthamstow–Highbury extension of the Victoria Line was opened. Its opening had a considerable effect on houses prices. (*Daily Mail*)

SEPTEMBER 2ND

1666: On this Sunday a fire broke out in the bakery of Thomas Faryner in Pudding Lane. Because it was the very early hours of a Sunday morning and no one worked in the Billingsgate area, the fire spread quickly, helped by a strong wind. It died out by the fifth day with at least 13,000 houses destroyed and ninety-four places of worship gutted.

1752: On this day the Calendar Revisions Act of 1751 stipulated that the following day would be 14 September! England had up until then been too severely Protestant to change from the Julian Calendar (when the year started on 25 March – Lady Day) to the Gregorian Calendar, when the year starts on 1 January.

1826: Bartholomew's Fair started with a woman sword sallower, a glass blower, a dwarf lady, rattlesnakes, and large and small crocodiles, as well as stalls for food and beverages. (*Morning Post*)

SEPTEMBER 3RD

1189: On this day Richard I, 'the Lionheart', was crowned in Westminster Abbey.

———•◆•———

1878: On this Tuesday at about 7.40 p.m., the *Princess Alice*, a saloon steamer carrying about 800 people, mostly women and children, was rammed and sunk by the *Bywell Castle*, a screw steamer, in Gallon's Reach, just below Woolwich on the Thames. Approximately 146 people were saved, sixteen of which died later. About 640 bodies were later recovered near Woolwich.

———•◆•———

1939: At 11.15 a.m. on this day, the Prime Minister, Neville Chamberlain, told the nation that it was at war with Germany.

On this Sunday, the first air-raid siren of the war sounded, but it was a false alarm, sparked by a French civilian airplane.

———•◆•———

1980: Peter O'Toole opened as 'Macbeth' at the Old Vic Theatre in Bryan Forbes' production. It was panned by critics, but loved by audiences.

SEPTEMBER 4TH

1909: Robert Baden-Powell organised the first rally for all Scouts at Crystal Palace on this Saturday; 11,000 boys attended, as did a number of girls dressed in uniform and calling themselves girl scouts. This led to the founding of the Girl Guides in 1910. (*The Times*)

1930: The Cambridge Theatre in Earlham Street opened on this day with André Charlot's revue *Masquerade* starring Beatrice Lillie. The theatre was built in steel and concrete and its interior was designed by Serge Chermayeff of Waring & Gillow. (English Heritage)

1954: In the Court at Greenwich a girl 'bridegroom' who married another girl at a white wedding in church was fined £25, as was her 'bride'. The 'bridegroom', twenty-six-year-old Violet Ellen Katherine Jones and the 'bride', twenty-one-year-old Joan Mary Lee of Ardgowan Road, Catford, both admitted making a false statement to get a marriage certificate. Violet Jones wore men's clothes – a fawn raincoat and trousers. (*The Times*)

September 5th

1538: After the split with Rome, Thomas Cromwell, Vicar-General for Henry VIII, introduced a scheme where each parish must keep a book, and that on Sundays, the incumbent, in the presence of the warders, must enter all baptisms, marriages and burials of the previous week. Failure to comply brought a fine that was to be spent on the upkeep of the Church. The order was largely ignored. This 'Mandate' was issued from White Hall.

———◆———

1975: Two people were killed and sixty-three injured when a suspected IRA bomb exploded in the lobby of the Hilton Hotel on Park Lane. A warning was sent to the *Daily Mail* just before midday, but the police were unable to evacuate the building before it exploded just after 12.15 p.m. (*Daily Mail*)

———◆———

1979: The naval gun carriage carrying the body of Earl Mountbatten, complete with the cocked hat of an Admiral of the Fleet, sword of honour and gold stick laid on top of the coffin, proceeded today from Wellington Barracks to Westminster Abbey. It was accompanied by the Royal Marine Bands and the Royal Family. (*The Times*)

SEPTEMBER 6TH

1828: The Gothic House for llamas at the London Zoo 'is one of the most picturesque … it contains two llamas, one of which was presented to the Society by the Duke of Bedford'. (*Mirror*)

—◆—

1889: A letter to the Editor of *The Times*, of this date, points out the inconvenience to a gentleman walking down a street pavement, wearing a customary hat, who will have his hat knocked off by the awning rods of shopkeepers. A further inconvenience is at night when lamps are hung outside shops at the same unreasonable height as to occasion further damage to headwear.

—◆—

1921: An inquest into the death of retired cook Joseph Eneckel, aged sixty-three, of Shepherd's Place Buildings, Mayfair, established that he had shot himself because he had hiccoughs for forty-eight hours and wanted to stop them. He had left a note, in French, to this effect. (*The Times*)

—◆—

1997: Diana, Princess of Wales' funeral was held at Westminster Abbey. An estimated 2.2 billion people worldwide watched the broadcast.

SEPTEMBER 7TH

1533: Elizabeth Tudor was born at Greenwich Palace on this day, to Henry VIII and Anne Boleyn. Both parents were sure that the child would be a boy. A document had already been prepared to this effect, and when Elizabeth was born an 's' was added to the word 'prince'. (Royal Museums, Greenwich)

1915: On this day the 7th Zeppelins attacked South London with the loss of sixteen lives, and East London where another sixteen were killed. (*Daily Mail*)

1931: The Granada Cinema in Tooting, Broadway, opened on this day. It was the first cinema to be preserved and given a Grade I listing. The marble interior, hall of mirrors and sumptuous décor was designed by Theodor Komisarjevsky. Fred Astaire performed there. It is now a bingo hall.

1940: On this day the German air force unleashed a wave of heavy bombing raids towards the end of the afternoon. About 300 bombs targeted the East End. A second wave of bombers came over at 11.30 p.m. The night bombing lasted over eight hours. (*The Times*)

September 8th

1915: The first bomb to fall on the City of London was on Fenchurch Street. The same day aeroplanes chased a Zeppelin all over London. (*The Times*)

1920: Victor Grayson, Labour MP for Colne Valley, walked out of the Georgian Restaurant in Chandos Place and was never seen again. Maundy Gregory, the confidence trickster, was suspected of his disappearance. It may have been that Grayson contrived his own disappearance under the strain of alcoholism and homosexuality. (*Daily Mail*)

1944: On this Friday the first V2 long-range rocket fell on Chiswick. Altogether 1,050 rockets reached Britain, killing 2,754 people and injuring 6,523. In this instance three people were killed.

1948: Terrence Rattigan's *The Browning Version* was first performed at the Phoenix with Eric Portman in the lead. It was an immediate success. (*The Times*)

1961: The gallows at Wandsworth Prison's E Wing were used for the last time on this day to hang Henryk Niemasz.

SEPTEMBER 9TH

1835: Bear-baiting and other forms of animal baiting such as dog-fighting had been popular for centuries. The best known arena for bear-baiting was the Bear Garden in London. Finally on this day the Cruelty to Animals Act was enacted. (*The Times*)

———◆———

1850: After Wordsworth's death in this year, there was talk of abolishing the post of Poet Laureate. Some suggested a woman such as Elizabeth Barrett Browning. Wordsworth's own choice suggested that Alfred Tennyson take the post, which he did on this day. (*The Times*)

———◆———

1911: On this Saturday afternoon Mr Gustav Hamel conveyed a bag of mail a distance of some twenty miles in fifteen minutes, but he was the only aviator of four who reached Windsor from Hendon. (*Windsor, Slough & Eton Express*)

———◆———

1970: Leila Khaled, a twenty-four-year-old Palestinian hijacker, spent her third night in the detention room at Ealing police station, despite protracted negotiations between the government and Arab guerrillas. She had been involved in an unsuccessful attempt to seize an El Al Boeing 747 at Heathrow. (*The Times*)

SEPTEMBER 10TH

1897: George Smith, a London taxi driver, drove into the frontage of a building in Bond Street and became the first person in the UK to be charged with drink-driving. He was fined £1. He admitted to having two or three glasses of beer. (*The Times*)

1940: At 3 a.m. a delayed action bomb fell on Regent Street near Piccadilly Circus. It exploded the following evening.

1963: The American Express credit card came to London and the UK on this day. It was the first credit card in the country and could be used in a wide range of outlets all over the world. (*The Times*)

1987: The former London County Council and the Greater London Council operated a blanket ban on hypnotism on stage, based on the 1952 Hypnotism Act. On this day Andrew Newton was permitted to perform hypnosis on stage at Wyndhams Theatre, for fourteen weeks, thereby breaking a thirty-five-year-old ban. (*Telegraph*)

September 11th

1940: On this day 180 Luftwaffe bombers hit East London.

———◆———

1978: Georgi Markov (1929-1978), the Bulgarian dissident and writer, died of suspected ricin poisoning in hospital on this day. Mr Markov had felt a strange prick of pain in his leg as a stranger had bumped into him on Waterloo Bridge on the 7th. His health deteriorated rapidly within the next few days. It is suspected that the poison was delivered via the point of an umbrella. (*Daily Telegraph*)

———◆———

1980: A 26-carat diamond, the 'Marlborough Diamond', was stolen by two Chicago gangsters from the Graff jewellers shop in Knightsbridge. They got away with a total of £1,429,000 worth of gems and were arrested in Chicago as they stepped off the plane. The diamond was never recovered. (*Daily Mail*)

———◆———

2003: A permanent memorial garden to those who lost their lives in the terrorist attacks in the United States on 11 September 2001 was built on behalf of the British government, in Grosvenor Square. Its opening was today. (*The Times*)

September 12th

1773: A writer to the *London Magazine* mentioned in ill-disguised contempt that 'our emaciated youth, who shattered by green tea and claret, drag their delicate and enervated forms at noon through Hyde Park where their ruddy forefathers were want to exhibit their manly forms'.

———◆———

1846: Robert Browning and Elizabeth Barrett were secretly married on this day at St Marylebone Parish Church. Elizabeth's furious father disinherited her. He disinherited all his children who married. (Marriage Registers)

———◆———

1878: After much debate over where it should be positioned, the original plan to place 'Cleopatra's Needle' outside Parliament was rejected. Instead it was placed in a position on the Embankment, where on this day the obelisk, commissioned by Pharoah Thutmose III, was unveiled. (*Engineering & Technology Magazine*)

———◆———

1907: Bertram Shaw, a dining-car cook with Midland Railway, returned to his flat at 29 St Paul's Road, Camden Town, where he and his fiancée Emily Dimmock lived. The flat was locked. He borrowed a key, only to find Emily dead, with her throat cut. (*Daily Mail*)

September 13th

1958: Collins's Music Hall on Islington Green was badly damaged by fire. Enough remained unscathed for talk of its rebuilding, but this never happened. (*The Times*)

1971: A massive theft of more than £3 million worth of jewels, cash and private papers from the vaults of Lloyds Bank on Baker Street was only reported on this day, despite the theft having been committed the previous Saturday. A 'D' notice stopped all further media coverage from Thursday 16 September. It was the largest ever bank robbery in the UK. Four men were jailed in 1973 and Michael X was hanged for a related murder in Trinidad. (*Daily Telegraph*)

2004: A protester representing the 'Fathers 4 Justice Campaign' dressed as 'Batman' broke into the grounds of Buckingham Palace. He was brought down from a balcony by police eight hours later. (*Mirror*)

2011: The House of Commons Culture, Media and Sports Select Committee announced its intention to recall James Murdoch in its probe into the News International phone hacking scandal.

September 14th

1865: On this day the 'Idol's Eye' diamond, a blue/white Golconda diamond, appeared at Christie's sale, described as a 'splendid large diamond, set round with 18 smaller brilliants'. It was sold to a mysterious buyer, 'B.B.'. (*Daily Telegraph*)

———•◆•———

1914: The first recruitment campaign for the First World War began with a grand assembly at the Guildhall. (*The Times*)

———•◆•———

1928: On this day PCs John Clayton and Charles Stevens were found guilty of perverting the course of justice by agreeing to prepare a false charge against the twenty-one-year-old Helen Adele of Islington. She had refused to sleep with Constable Clayton and they had arrested her on a false charge. Both were sentenced to eighteen months' imprisonment. (*The Times*)

———•◆•———

1974: Chia Chia and Ching Ching, a pair of giant pandas presented to Prime Minister Edward Heath during his visit to China, arrived in London on this day. (*The Times*)

September 15th

1874: Vincenzo Lunardi, Secretary to the Italian Ambassador, made the first ascent in London in a balloon from the Royal Artillery Grounds. He had a dog, a cat and a pigeon for company. He touched down at North Mimms, Hertfordshire. The first balloon ascent in Great Britain, however, was by a Scot, Tytler, near Edinburgh on 24 July! (*General Advertiser*)

1940: On this day there were two major Luftwaffe attacks on London and whilst some turned away when confronted by Spitfire and Hurricane squadrons, Buckingham Palace was hit. Continued raids during the day ensured that railway bridges were hit between Victoria and Clapham Junction, as well as the railway at East Croydon. (*The Times*)

1964: The *Sun*, with the slogan 'a paper born of the age we live in', was launched as a replacement for the defunct *Daily Herald*.

1988: The Museum of the Moving Image, the MOMI, sited by the South Bank Centre, was opened by Prince Charles. (*Evening Standard*)

September 16th

1841: Since the previous Saturday, the residents of Sutton Court House, Sutton Lane, Chiswick, had been in a continued state of alarm due to windows of the mansion being continually broken by some unknown agent. Every method adopted for detecting the party guilty of the outrage failed in its object. (*The Times*)

1940: On this day a high-explosive bomb demolished Savile Row, damaging adjacent properties. Surrounding windows were shattered and a coal gas leak was then discovered. (*The Times*)

1967: The Prom audience at the Royal Albert Hall bade farewell to Sir Malcolm Sargent. He died three weeks later.

1977: At 4 a.m. a car driven by the American singer Gloria Jones with passenger Marc Bolan, the former T-Rex singer, crashed in Barnes, killing Bolan and injuring Miss Jones. They had been travelling back to his home in Richmond from a Mayfair restaurant. (*Daily Mail*)

SEPTEMBER 17TH

1091: A tornado, now thought to have been of 200mph strength, hit London, badly damaging London Bridge, levelling the church of St Mary-le-Bow. About 600 wooden houses in the city were flattened. (City of London Records Office)

1940: From this night until 3 November the Luftwaffe bombed London every night.

1944: V2 bombs landed in Lewisham, affecting railway lines and destroying houses.

1945: In the Central Criminal Court at the Old Bailey, before Mr Justice Tucker and a jury, William Joyce (aka Lord Haw-Haw) was charged with three counts of high treason. (*The Times*)

1993: The British National Party won its first council seat, a marginal seat in Millwall, East London. Derek Beackton, an unemployed lorry driver beat the Labour candidate by seven votes. Politicians on all sides deplored the result, which showed the BNP's share of the vote rise to 33.9 per cent. (*East London Advertiser*)

SEPTEMBER 18TH

1714: King George I of Hanover arrived in Britain for the first time, landing in Greenwich.

———◆———

1954: Archaeologists excavating a bomb-site behind the Mansion House in the City discovered the vestiges of a third-century Roman temple dedicated to the cult of Mithras. The temple remains were removed and reconstructed in front of what is now Bucklersbury House. (*The Times*)

———◆———

1966: The 'Notting Hill Fayre', the brainchild of Mrs Laslett, opened for the first time on this Sunday. There was a parade consisting of a man dressed as Henry VIII and children as Charles Dickens characters, an Afro-Cuban band, an Orleans-style marching band, a Trinidadian steel band and the London Irish Pipers. It lasted for three days. The Notting Hill Carnival continues to this day. (*West London Observer*)

———◆———

1970: Jimi Hendrix, the rock guitarist, collapsed during a party at a house in Landsdowne Crescent, Notting Hill Gate, and was taken to St Mary Abbot's Hospital where he was found to be dead. (*Daily Express*)

SEPTEMBER 19TH

1960: The very first parking ticket to be issued by parking wardens, introduced on this day in central London, was to a Dr Creighton, who was answering an emergency call to a West End Hotel – 343 others received fines on this day. (*The Standard*)

1972: Dr Ami Sachori, a diplomat at the Israeli Embassy in London, was killed by a parcel bomb. The bomb was one of eight sent to the embassy, but the other seven were detected before they could do any harm. (*The Times*)

1997: The Intercity 125 from Swansea to London ploughed into a freight train at Southall, killing six and injuring more than 150. The enquiry ruled that the driver had been negligent by not stopping when two signals warned him of the freight train in front. The Automatic Warning System also failed to work. (*Daily Mail*)

2005: Ayman Al-Zawahri, the deputy leader of Al Quaeda, admitted that Al Quaeda had carried out the 7 July bombings on the London transport system. (*The Times*)

September 20th

1929: Clarence Hatry, an insurance broker and a successful forger, was arrested. He had worked out his greatest financial project, a merger of Steel and Iron (which would later become British Steel). He had not been able to raise the money so he faked some share certificates which gave him collateral for loans of £1.6 million. Just as the deal was about to be consummated, the fraud was discovered. The Hatry Group had until then been worth £24 million. Nine days later the Wall Street Crash began. The man with the second largest yacht in the world, a string of racehorses and luxury properties spent Christmas in Brixton Prison and was sentenced to fourteen years. (*The Times*)

————•+•————

1982: Two black youths mugged a woman near Pym House, Brixton, and stabbed a Ghanaian barrister, Malik Ownsu, when he came to help her. He died soon after. (*The Times*)

————•+•————

1991: A 170ft crane crashed through the roof of the church of St James Garlickhythe in the City, its counterbalance smashing through the church's roof window. The Wren church had survived the Second World War virtually unscathed. (*The Times*)

SEPTEMBER 21ST

1875: Henry Wainwright, a married shopkeeper with a house in Tredegar Square, met Harriet Lane in 1871 and set her up as his mistress at St Peter's Street in Mile End. She had two children by him. By 1874 Henry was facing financial ruin and decided to get rid of his mistress. In June 1875, being bankrupt, Henry got rid of his shop and asked a youth to carry some parcels for him – a hand fell out of one! On this day Henry was charged with her murder and hanged at Newgate in December, whilst his brother, an accessory, was sent to prison. (*The Times*)

1991: Twenty-four-year-old Michael Watson, the super middleweight up-and-coming boxer, fought Chris Eubank in June 1991 at Earl's Court. Eubank won. A rematch was arranged for this day at White Hart Lane for the vacant WBO super middleweight title. In round 4 Eubank delivered a devastating uppercut. Watson collapsed in round 12, suffered brain damage and spent over a year in intensive care. This ended his career. (*Independent*)

SEPTEMBER 22ND

1735: On this day Sir Robert Walpole moved into 10 Downing Street. It was gifted to him by King George II. Walpole had also commissioned the architect William Kent to join the house with the other behind it. (*Victoria County Histories*)

1809: On this day Theodore Hook (1788-1841), one of the most celebrated improvisators of the English language, celebrated his twenty-first birthday. He had already written nine shows performed in the West End – a record which has never been surpassed. (*The Times*)

1848: John Harrold, a seaman newly arrived from Hamburg and residing at No. 8 New Lane, Gainsford Street, Horsleydown, Southwark, was seized with cholera and died in a few hours. This was the first undoubted case of cholera in the capital according to Dr Parkes of the Health Board. (John Snow Society)

1920: On this day the Mobile Patrol Experiment (the Flying Squad), a reorganisation of a previous police department, was formed under Commissioner Sir Nevil Macready. (*The Official History of the Metropolitan Police*, Gary Mason)

SEPTEMBER 23RD

1518: On this day the College of Physicians was granted a Charter. This granted sole power to license physicians in London and for seven miles around. (City of London Records Office)

1897: Stephen Kempton, a nine-year-old cadging a ride by standing on the back springs of a Bersey, was crushed to death in the West End when his coat got caught in the driving chain. He was the first child car fatality in Britain. (*The Times*)

1952: The actor and director Charlie Chaplin and his wife Oona returned to London for the first time in twenty-one years. (*Guardian*)

1957: The Central School of Speech and Drama, founded by Elsie Fogerty in 1906 at the Royal Albert Hall, moved to the Embassy Theatre in Swiss Cottage. (*Daily Telegraph*)

1959: Westland Aircraft opened Battersea Heliport between Battersea and Wandsworth Bridges. It was the first heliport in the country. (*Daily Mail*)

SEPTEMBER 24TH

1842: A bronze effigy of the Duke of Wellington on his horse, Copenhagen, was conveyed to the Green Park Arch on this day. (*The Times*)

————•————

1888: The present Royal Court Theatre in Sloane Square was opened on this day as the 'New Court Theatre'. It was used as a cinema from 1935-40 until bomb damage closed it. (*The Times*)

————•————

1917: On this day thirteen people were killed and twenty-two injured on the steps of the Old Bedford Hotel, Southampton Row, by a 121lb bomb dropped by a Gotha in one of London's first night raids. (plaque, WC1)

————•————

1992: Cabinet Minister David Mellor resigned, following his affair with Antonia de Sancha, an actress and businesswoman who had also played the part of a prostitute in a film *The Pieman*! The *Sun* reported that Mellor had asked to make love to de Sancha wearing a replica Chelsea Football Club shirt.

September 25th

1660: On this day Samuel Pepys, having worked at his office discussing international politics, noted that, 'Afterwards I did send for a cup of tee, a China drink, of which I had never drunk before'. This may have been the first time a Londoner mentioned such refreshment.

———◆———

1818: James Blundell, an obstetrician at Guy's Hospital, carried out the first human blood transfusion on a cachectic man dying of cancer of the stomach. The man's condition improved for some hours, but he died fifty-six hours later. (*British Medical Journal*)

———◆———

1906: John Galsworthy's *Silver Box* premiered at the Royal Court Theatre, establishing him as a dramatic force. The play strived to gain dramatic effect from social situations rather than from character. (*The Times*)

———◆———

2003: The Hutton Enquiry heard the final arguments into the death of Dr David Kelly. The Kelly family criticised the Ministry of Defence and the government attacked the BBC. After six weeks of evidence Lord Hutton absolved the government of any kind of 'dishonourable, underhand or duplicitous strategy'. (*The Times*)

September 26th

1769: Honoretta Pratt was illegally burnt in an open grave at St George's burial ground, Hanover Square. An inscription on a stone beside her grave explains the reason for this first recorded cremation in England.

1816: The Revd John Church, long suspected of involvement in a male brothel in Vere Street, Clare Market, was indicted at the Surrey Assizes, Croydon, for attempting sodomy upon a young man of his congregation. The nineteen-year-old apprentice potter, Adam Foreman, alleged that Church had entered his room one night, had placed a hand on his genitals and feigned the voice of his mistress. Upon the discovery of the ruse, Foreman fled. Church was eventually found guilty in August 1817. (*The Times*)

1965: On this day Queen Elizabeth II appointed four members of the Beatles, John Lennon, Paul McCartney, Ringo Starr and George Harrison, as ' Members of the British Empire'. They would be given their MBEs at Buckingham Palace on 26 October.

1970: Outline planning consent for a £6 million airport terminal at Hammersmith was granted by the Minister of Housing. The project was opposed, though, by the Greater London Council. (*The Times*)

SEPTEMBER 27TH

1885: *Lloyds Weekly London Newspaper* reported that the Bow Street Police Court was thronged with an eager and expectant crowd over the preliminary hearing on the Armstrong case, in which Mr Stead, the newspaper editor, stood accused of abduction and indecent assault on a minor. Amongst others present were Mrs Josephine Butler, Miss Emma Booth, Mr Bramwell Booth and others.

———•—•———

1940: By this day a London Transport Survey estimated that 177,000 people were sheltering in seventy-nine underground stations.

———•—•———

1960: Bank Station had been opened by 1898 and the only exit was a sloping corridor. The 1930s saw a series of plans for narrow travelling footways shelved. The Second World War and austerity stopped any further ideas until the late 1950s, and finally construction got underway in 1957. Europe's first travelator was ceremonially unveiled on this day. (London Underground Archives)

———•—•———

1968: A day after censorship was abolished on stage, the musical *Hair*, featuring thirteen naked actors, opened at the Shaftsbury Theatre. (*The Times*)

SEPTEMBER 28TH

1666: Robert Hubert, a Frenchman, was hanged at Tyburn for confessing to starting the Great Fire of London, although he was not there at the time! (City of London Records Office)

◆

1731: A cricket match between Surrey and London was played at Kennington Common. Frederick, Prince of Wales, a major patron, attended.

◆

1928: 'One sometimes finds what one is not looking for. When I woke up after dawn today I certainly didn't plan to revolutionise medicine by discovering the world's first antibiotic' – which is what Alexander Fleming and his team did on this day at St Mary's Hospital, Paddington.

◆

1985: On Saturday morning the police, whilst looking for a suspect, shot Mrs Groce of Brixton in her own home. This was the catalyst for that evening's riot in Brixton. It lasted four days, resulting in ninety burglaries, 107 motor vehicle offences and 285 other incidents; 30 per cent of the rioters were white, 70 per cent black, and 1,500 police officers were deployed. (*The Times*)

September 29th

1399: On this day Richard II, King of England, an emotional, hot-tempered and illogical monarch, resigned the Crown in London – being deposed by Parliament the next day, in favour of the Duke of Lancaster, the future Henry IV. (*Oxford Dictionary of National Biography*)

1792: St Patrick's Roman Catholic church, Soho Square, was consecrated on this day. It was the first church in England since the Reformation to be dedicated to St Patrick. The present church was built between 1891-93, but it stands on where Carlisle House once was. Mrs Cornelys, a Venetian courtesan and one of Casanova's many lovers, owned it in 1766.

1829: On this Tuesday the first metropolitan policeman went out on duty from the still unfinished station house in Scotland Yard. (*The Times*)

1999: The first part of the Jubilee extension was opened between Bermondsey and Canary Wharf. (*The Times*)

SEPTEMBER 30TH

1737: The Fleet Market, built over the culverted Fleet River (now Farringdon Street), opened with a central row of shops and a market building with a clock tower. (City of London Records Office)

1840: Today the first stone of Nelson's Column was laid by Charles Davison Scott at a ceremony conducted 'in a private manner, owing to the workmen and gentlemen, comprising the committee being absent from town'. (*Nautical Magazine*)

1937: The last edition of the *Morning Post* was published on this day. It was then merged with the *Daily Telegraph*.

1959: The last private passenger aeroplane left Croydon Airport at 6.15 p.m. The airport officially closed at 10.30 p.m. (*The Times*)

1967: BBC Radio 1 was launched at 7 a.m. with Tony Blackburn's Breakfast Show.

1971: Oleg Lyalin, a member of the Russian Trade Delegation in London, due to appear at a London Magistrate's court on this day for a driving offence, was named by the government as the Soviet defector who had the previous week exposed dozens of Russians alleged to be spying in the UK. (*The Times*)

OCTOBER 1ST

1677: In this month a 'directory of London Merchants' was brought out by Richard L'Estrange. This was the first *London Directory*. (City of London Records Office)

———◆———

1792: On this day the Baptist Missionary Society was formed in London.

———◆———

1859: On this Saturday the Great Bell of Westminster sounded for the last time and, while in the very act of striking, Big Ben became dumb forever. The bell was even more hopelessly cracked than its predecessor and it was claimed that, like him, too, it must be broken up and re-cast before the great clock of the metropolis could again record the flight of time. (*The Times*)

———◆———

1868: The Midland Railway Station, St Pancras, was opened on this day to little ceremony. George Gilbert Scott designed the Gothic station frontage. The single-span elliptical overall roof, the largest known such structure in the world at the time, was designed by W.H. Barlow and R.H. Ordish – this allowed the station below to make maximum use of space without obstruction. (*The Times*)

OCTOBER 2ND

1899: The first two motorised double-decker buses ran this Monday, from Victoria to Kennington Park – and they were red! (*The Times*)

1907: Hampstead Garden Suburb was opened. It was founded by the philanthropist Henrietta Barnett and her husband Canon Barnett with a Utopian idea in mind of creating a suburb to cater for all classes of people and all income groups. The church St Jude's was designed by Edwin Lutyens and the gardens by Richard Unwin, amongst others. (*The Times*)

1909: The first match was held at Twickenham Rugby Ground between Richmond and Harlequins on this day. Twickenham is affectionately known as the 'cabbage patch', because the grounds were originally used to grow cabbages. The first international England *v.* Wales game was played in 1910; at that time the seating the seating capacity was 20,000 – now it is over 80,000. (*Daily Mail*)

1973: The church of the Holy Trinity in Trinity Square was gutted by fire. It was renovated and converted into music rehearsal rooms. (*Evening Standard*)

OCTOBER 3RD

1888: The premiere of the operetta *Yeoman of the Guard* by W.S. Gilbert and A. Sullivan was held at the Savoy Theatre on this day. It ran for 423 performances, and critics thought the score Sullivan's finest, including the overture. This was also the first Savoy Opera to use Sullivan's larger orchestra. Most of Sullivan's subsequent operas used this larger orchestra. (*The Times*)

1929: The Dominion Theatre in Tottenham Court Road opened. It was a cinema within three years. It was built on the site of the former Horse Shoe Brewery, the site of the 1814 London Beer Flood. (*Daily Mail*)

1956: The Bolshoi Ballet appeared for the first time in London at the Royal Opera House. (*The Times*)

1975: Six remaining hostages, held by armed gunmen in the cellars of a Knightsbridge restaurant, were released unharmed after five days. Their troubles had started when staff were collecting £13,000 of the week's takings and three men burst in. One of the staff managed to escape and alert the authorities. (*Daily Mail*)

OCTOBER 4TH

1875: The Detective and Public Carriage Department took possession of the new police offices at Great Scotland Yard. (Police Archives)

———◆———

1911: Earl's Court escalator, the first commercial underground escalator, was unveiled. The LER employed one of their staff, 'Bumper' Harris, a clerk of works, to ride the escalators to demonstrate their safety. He had, unfortunately, a wooden leg and both the media and the passengers wondered if he lost the leg on the escalator. (*The Times*)

———◆———

1936: On this Sunday morning Oswald Moseley led 3,000 blackshirts into the East End from the Royal Mint, protected by 7,000 police. At Cable Street a large barrier was erected by locals. After scuffles broke out the police decided it was unsafe for the fascists to continue. A victory for the East End! (*The Times*)

———◆———

1976: British Rail started its high-speed train service on this day, called the Inter-city service, with a potential speed of 140mph. The first train left Paddington station at 8.06 a.m. and arrived in Bristol three minutes early. (*Daily Mail*)

OCTOBER 5TH

1518: On this day an infant of barely six months, François Dauphin of France, was 'married' at Greenwich today to the almost as young Mary, daughter of Henry VIII and Catherine of Aragon. A ring was placed on her finger. The arrangement was abandoned in 1520. She would become Mary, Queen of England; the Dauphin would die, possibly of tuberculosis, in 1536. (*Who's Who in Tudor England*, C.R.N. Routh and Peter Holmes)

———◆———

1983: Cecil Parkinson, Secretary of State for Trade and Industry, admitted to an affair with his former secretary, Sara Keays. (*The Times*)

———◆———

1999: A Thames train left Paddington station on this morning and collided with a First Great Western train from Cheltenham at Ladbroke Grove. Thirty-one people, including the drivers of both trains involved, were killed; 227 people were admitted to hospital and 296 people were treated for minor injuries at the site of the crash. It was the worst accident on the Great Western Main Line and was subject to a lengthy inquiry that resulted in large financial penalties and new Rail Standards and Guidelines. (*Evening Standard*)

OCTOBER 6TH

1216: On this day the Tower of London finally opened its gates to Louis 'the Lion' of France, ending its neutrality and accepting his suzerainty. (*Blood Cries Afar,* Sean McGlynn)

———◆———

1985: A large police raid on Broadwater Farm Estate in Tottenham looking for drug dealers resulted in riots by young black people. PC Keith Blakelock was hacked to death. The local MP Bernie Grant said, 'the locals believed the police were to blame … and what they got was a bloody good hiding'. (*Guardian*)

———◆———

2007: Jason Lewis, a self-powered navigator, ended his thirteen-year circumnavigation of the Earth at Greenwich. He and a friend, Stevie Smith, cycled, roller-bladed, kayaked, hiked and pedalled across the globe. He is accredited as the first person to circumnavigate the globe by human power. (*Daily Telegraph*)

OCTOBER 7TH

1857: Charles Spurgeon, the most influential Victorian Baptist preacher, addressed the largest crowd in his ministry, 23,654 at the Crystal Palace, Sydenham. He noted that, 'a day or two before preaching, I went to decide where the platform should be fixed; and in order to test the acoustic properties of the building, cried in a loud voice, "Behold the Lamb of God, which taketh away the sins of the World". A workman working in one of the galleries, who knew nothing of what was being done, heard the words, and they came like a message to his soul. He was smitten with conviction on account of sin, put down his tools, went home, and thereafter a season of spiritual struggling, found peace.' (*Memoirs*)

———◆———

1986: The *Independent* newspaper was first published as a broadsheet in London. It was produced by Newspaper Publishing Plc., and was created by Andreas Whittam Smith, Stephen Glover and Brett Straub, former journalists at the *Daily Telegraph*. It challenged the *Guardian* for centre-left readers and sparked a general freshening of the British press, design and price war.

OCTOBER 8TH

1831: King's College was opened at a ceremony attended by the Duke of Wellington, archbishops and thirty bishops. (*The Times*)

———◆◆———

1871: The clergyman and headmaster of Stockwell grammar school, Mr John Selby Watson, murdered his virago of a wife, Anne, at their house at No. 28 St Martin's Road, Stockwell. Despite the Judge's ruling that he be hanged, he was given life imprisonment. The media of the day thought the fact that he was a man of the cloth changed the ruling. (*Daily Telegraph*)

———◆◆———

1952: At 8.18 a.m. the overnight express sleeper travelling from Perth to Euston overshot the signals at Harrow and ploughed into a stationary local train waiting at the station. Soon after, a northbound express from Euston ran into the wreckage, causing carnage in the station crowded with commuters – 120 people were killed and 150 people injured. (*Daily Mail*)

———◆◆———

1965: The iconic Post Office Tower, topped by a revolving restaurant, became operational. It was opened to the public a year later. (*Daily Telegraph*)

OCTOBER 9TH

1878: Wandsworth Prison's first execution was that of Thomas Smithers for the murder of his 'common-law' wife. His executioner, William Marwood, was credited with developing the long-drop method which broke the culprit's neck, rather than causing death by a slow strangulation. (*The Times*)

1975: An IRA bomb exploded at about 9 p.m. at a bus stop near Green Park tube station and the Ritz Hotel on Piccadilly. The explosion knocked pedestrians off their feet and shattered shop windows, blowing cars across the pavement. Graham Tuck, a twenty-three-year-old vagrant, was severely wounded and died of his wounds at St George's Hospital, Hyde Park. At least twenty-three people were injured by flying glass. (*Evening Standard*)

1988: On this day Igor Judge was appointed to the Queen's Bench division of the High Court of Justice and awarded a knighthood. (Register)

1991: The Royal Albert Hall staged the first sumo wrestling tournament outside of Japan. Spectators paid in excess of £100 to get some of the best seats. (*Daily Telegraph*)

OCTOBER 10TH

1354: On this day Edward III settled *6d* per day for life on Coursus de Gangeland 'Apothecaries Londoni', for taking care of him during his severe illness in Scotland. (City of London Records Office)

————•◆•————

1677: On this day Sir Thomas Grosvenor married the twelve-year-old Mary Davies, heiress of 100 acres of what is now Mayfair and 400 acres of what is now Belgravia and Pimlico – which was marshland! (Register)

————•◆•————

1926: The first London mosque, at Melrose Road, Southfields, was opened by Khan Bahadur Shaikh Abdul Qadir, president of the Punjab Legislative Council. (*The Times*)

————•◆•————

1940: A bomb hit the former residence of the King and Queen when Duke and Duchess of York, No. 145 Piccadilly. On this same night and throughout it, 400 bombs hit London, destroying main-line stations, hitting Battersea Power Station, the BBC at Portland Place and Leicester Square; in all there were 1,000 fires. (*The Times*)

OCTOBER 11TH

1821: Sir George Williams was born. Initially a buyer for Hitchcock Rogers & Co., a large draper at No. 72 St Paul's churchyard, he became a partner on marrying the firm's head, and was one of the original founders in 1844 of what was to become the YMCA. (*Oxford Dictionary of National Biography*)

1870: The hangman William Calcroft hanged Margaret Waters at Horsemonger Lane Gaol. It was Calcraft's first private hanging. She was the first baby farmer to be executed and this had been the first baby farming case to come before the Courts. (*The Times*)

1919: The Hammersmith Palais de Danse was opened at Shepherd's Bush Road – it closed in 2007. Once billed as the most famous spot in the world, it profoundly influenced the European dance scene for over sixty years. (*Daily Mail*)

1949: The Tennesee Williams play *A Streetcar Named Desire* opened at the Aldwych Theatre. Vivienne Leigh played the lead and Laurence Olivier was the producer. Queues started twenty-four hours beforehand! (*The Times*)

OCTOBER 12TH

1537: Henry VIII was desperate for a son as there was a vital perceived need to continue the dynasty. Accordingly, Henry divorced Catherine of Aragon, then had Anne Boleyn executed for not bearing him a son. Finally Janey Seymour, his third wife, produced him an heir, Edward, at Hampton Court Palace on this day.

———◆———

1884: The underground station 'The Tower of London' at the site of the present 'Tower Hill Station' closed on this day, when the nearby station at Mark Lane opened. It had only been in existence for two years. It had been opened during the construction of the Metropolitan Line, but it was decided that when the Circle Line was created a larger station was required, and so Mark Lane was built as a replacement. (*The Times*)

———◆———

1974: The UK's first branch of McDonalds opened in Woolwich at No. 56-58 Powis Street and is still going strong! It was McDonalds' 3,000th restaurant. The company admitted that at first nobody went in. A burger then cost 18p and a 'Big Mac' was then called a 'Big Boy'. (*Kentish Independent*)

OCTOBER 13TH

1726: At about 9 p.m. the skies above a starlit London erupted into streaks of lights, turning into tongues of red, blue and white flames, finally converging into a large ball of light resembling the sun, then steadily dying out. (C. de Saussure)

1884: Greenwich was adopted as the initial meridian of Longitude, from which standard times throughout the world are calculated. (*The Times*)

1905: Emmeline Pankhurst and Annie Kenney, suffragette pioneers, both attended a meeting in London, to hear Sir Edward Grey, a government minister, talking. They constantly barracked him with 'Will the Liberal government give votes to women?' When they refused to stop, the police evicted them. In the struggle a policeman claimed he had been kicked by them. They were arrested and charged with assault. (*The Women's Suffrage Movement 1866-1928*)

1915: The Zeppelins struck London, bombing over Charing Cross, killing seventeen and injuring twenty. Bombs were also dropped on Holborn and the Zeppelin was fired at by a 75mm gun sited at the Honourable Artillery Co. (*Daily Telegraph*)

OCTOBER 14TH

1539: On this day the Augustine Priory of St Mary's Overie in Montague Close, by what is now known as Southwark Cathedral, was dissolved. (City of London Records Office)

1644: William Penn, advocate of religious and political freedom and founder of the colony of Pennsylvania, was born in the Liberty of the Tower of London. (*Oxford Dictionary of National Biography*)

1660: Maj.-Gen. Thomas Harrison, the seventeenth of the fifty-nine commissioners to sign King Charles I's death warrant in 1649, was the first person to be found guilty of regicide. He was the first regicide to be hanged, drawn and quartered. (Samuel Pepys)

1940: A bomb fell in the road above Balham tube station. The blast ruptured the water mains and sewage pipes, also penetrating into the underground line 9m below. Sixty-eight lives were lost. (*Wandsworth Guardian*)

1968: The Queen opened the new Euston station. It was spacious, but critics labelled it as characterless. (*The Times*)

October 15th

1702: On this day Lady Frances Stewart, a mistress of Charles II and model for the first portrait of Britannia, contracted smallpox and died shortly afterwards on this day.

———•—•———

1851: The Great Exhibition closed at Hyde Park. It would shortly be re-erected in Sydenham. (*The Times*)

———•—•———

1901: The Tooting Bec Trophy was inaugurated on this day. Awarded yearly by the PGA of Great Britain and Ireland to a UK member who returns the lowest single score in the Open Championship, it was originally presented at a thirty-six-hole stroke play tournament at the Tooting Bec (Furzedown) Golf Club. (PGA)

———•—•———

1940: A BBC newsreader carried on reading the news whilst Broadcasting House sustained a direct hit from a bomb. (*The Times*)

———•—•———

1962: Hyde Park underground car park opened with a novel automatic barrier and parking for 1,100 cars. (*Daily Telegraph*)

OCTOBER 16TH

1733: The now dilapidated church of St Luke's in Old Street was consecrated on this day. Its designer was John James, with strong help from Hawksmoor. (City of London Records Office)

———◆———

1793: John Hunter (1728-1793), the father of anatomy, died on this day of a heart attack during an argument at St George's Hospital, Hyde Park Corner, over the admission of students. His knowledge of anatomy was honed through years of dissecting corpses, provided by Resurrectionists. (*Oxford Dictionary of National Biography*)

———◆———

1834: Overheated chimney flues caused a fire in the Palace of Westminster, the home of Parliament. It spread rapidly through the mediaeval complex, gutting most of the palace. Westminster Hall was one of the few parts to survive intact, as well as the crypt under St Stephen's. (*The Times*)

———◆———

1940: At 3.30 p.m. a bomb fell on the south-west corner of Leicester Square, blowing it away. (*The Times*)

OCTOBER 17TH

1678: The skewered corpse of the magistrate Sir Edmund Berry Godfrey was found on the south side of Primrose Hill. Anti-Catholic feeling was rife, especially in the wake of Titus Oates. The murder of this judge was laid on three Catholics – his murderers, though, were never caught.

———◆·———

1814: The Dominion Theatre on Tottenham Court Road occupies the site of the Manx & Co. Brewery, demolished in 1922. On this day a huge vat at the brewery, containing 135,000 imperial gallons of beer, ruptured. This created a domino effect with the other vats. About 15 million litres of beer gushed into the street and into properties, destroying two houses and damaging the local Tavistock Arms Pub. This disaster killed seven. The Courts held that this was an Act of God. (*The Times*)

———◆·———

1892: On this day Thomas Neill Cream, a Canadian doctor living in the Waterloo area, was indicted for four murders and other crimes at the Old Bailey. (*The Times*)

———◆·———

1998: The former dictator of Chile, Gen. Pinochet, was arrested during private treatment at a London Hospital on a warrant from Spain requesting his extradition on murder charges. (*Daily Telegraph*)

OCTOBER 18TH

1660: On this day a proclamation forbade hackney carriages to ply their trade. This was ineffectual as Samuel Pepys picked one up on the same day! (Samuel Pepys)

———◆•———

1660: This was also St Luke's Day, the traditional day for the start of the Charlton Horn Fair, where everyone wore horns. It had an appalling reputation. Daniel Defoe said it was infamous for 'the rabble of rude people, which ought to be suppress'd … they take all kinds of liberties … the women give themselves up to all manner of indecency and immodesty'. It was suppressed under the Fairs Act of 1871.

———◆•———

1910: The trial of Dr Hawley Harvey Crippen for the murder of his wife, Cora, began at the Old Bailey. Had he pleaded guilty he might have escaped execution. As it was, the Jury only took twenty minutes to find him guilty. (*The Times*)

———◆•———

1966: On this day the Queen granted a Royal Pardon to Timothy Evans. Sixteen years earlier Evans had been charged with the murder of his daughter in Rillington Place. However, it was discovered that John Christie had committed the crime. (*The Times*)

OCTOBER 19TH

1704: From this day until 12 February 1705, 295 marriages were celebrated in the Fleet Prison without licence or banns. Twenty to thirty couples were sometimes married in a day, and their names concealed if they chose to pay extra. Painted signs of joined male and female hands inscribed 'marriages performed within' hung on the walls of the building. (City of London Records Office)

1739: Captain Jenkins produced his pickled ear before Parliament, claiming it was cut off by a Spaniard. On this day Walpole declared war on Spain.

1741: David Garrick first appeared on the London stage on this day as Richard III at Gifford's Theatre, originally Goodman's Fields Theatre in South Whitechapel. (*General Advertiser*)

1972: *Crown Matrimonial*, a play about the Abdication crisis of 1936, was first performed on this day at the Haymarket. Amanda Reiss portrayed the Queen Mother – the first portrayal of a living member of the Royal Family. (*The Times*)

OCTOBER 20TH

1708: St Paul's Cathedral was finally finished on this day. (City of London Records Office)

1862: Catherine Wilson, a suspected serial killer, was the last woman to be publicly hanged in London. (*The Times*)

1927: 'La Deliverance', a 16ft statue of a naked woman holding a sword aloft was unveiled on this day, at Henly's Corner at the bottom of Regent's Park Road. A gift from Lord Rothermere, the statue was created by Emile Guillaume to celebrate the Battle of the Marne in 1914. Ten other copies were made. (*The Times*)

1960: Today Penguin Books was prosecuted under the Obscene Publications Act, 1959, at the Old Bailey for publishing *Lady Chatterley's Lover* by D.H. Lawrence. (*The Times*)

1993: PC Patrick Dunne, aged forty-four, was shot dead in Cato Road, Clapham. He was attending a minor incident and ran out when he heard gunfire, only for a bullet to kill him. (*South London Press*)

OCTOBER 21ST

1848: A contributor to the *Lancet* reported that, 'many persons every morning drink of the many Hyde Park wells, or have the water brought home for other daily use'.

—— • —— • ——

1856: The Great Bell that would go on the Clock Tower by Parliament was delivered to Palace Yard on a dray pulled by sixteen horses – there it was unpacked. It was proposed to call this bell 'Big Ben' after Sir Benjamin Hall, the president of the Board of Works. (*The Times*)

—— • —— • ——

1935: Mrs Roy Fox was fined 40s at the Croydon County Police Court for landing at Croydon from abroad on 23 September 'a small dog, black and brown with a short tail'. KLM was similarly summoned and fined £5. Asked for the licence, Mrs Fox said that she understood that it had to be obtained on arriving. The dog was quarantined. Both Mrs Fox and KLM contravened the strict regulations on imported dogs. 'They might be carriers of rabies.' (*Manchester Guardian*)

OCTOBER 22ND

1910: Dr Hawley Crippen was convicted at the Old Bailey of the murder of his wife, Cora Elmore. Recent analysis of the remains that convicted him have been shown to be male. (*The Times*)

———◆·———

1966: The British double-agent, George Blake, escaped from Wormwood Scrubs, aided and abetted by three men, who thought a forty-two-year sentence was inhumane. He fled to Moscow. The wardens had last seen him at the evening roll call at 5.30 p.m. An hour-and-a-half later his cell was found empty. A window at the end of a corridor had had its bars sawn away. (*The Times*)

———◆·———

1974: A 5lb bomb left in the restaurant of Brooks' Club exploded after diners had left. Three waiters were treated for cuts and shock in hospital. Commander Robert Hardy of Scotland Yard said that there was always a possibility the bomb had been thrown through the windows. (*Daily Mail*)

1983: An estimated 1 million people took part today in a largely well-regulated Campaign for Nuclear Disarmament rally in Hyde Park. (*Daily Telegraph*)

OCTOBER 23RD

1731: The Cotton Library, the private library of the antiquarian Sir Robert Cotton, donated to the nation by his family, was housed in Ashburnham House in Little Dean's Yard, Westminster. On this day a fire broke out in the house and destroyed or damaged 114 of the 958 volumes. (*Daily Courant*)

———•◆•———

1843: On this day, fourteen of the stonemasons who had worked on Nelson's Column ate a celebratory meal on the platform, before the statue of Nelson was placed on it. Had Germany conquered Britain, Hitler had planned to ship the column back to Berlin, as the 'Nelson Column represents for Britain a symbol of British naval might and world domination. It would be an impressive way of underlining the German Victory …'. (*Daily Mail*)

———•◆•———

2010: The London Transport region of the RMT called for a march to support the TUC anti-cuts meeting on Tottenham Court Road. The march was supported by the London Fire Brigade Union, the Civil Service Union and the Teacher's Union. (*Socialist Newspaper*)

OCTOBER 24TH

1681: The Earl of Shaftsbury had been arrested on suspicion of high treason and was committed to the Tower of London. He moved for a writ of Habeas Corpus on this day. His case finally came before a Grand Jury on the 24 November 1681. The case against him was dropped due to insufficient evidence.

1908: On this day Emmeline and Christabel Pankhurst, mother and daughter, were sent to prison 'for inciting the public to rush the House of Commons'. Lloyd George, the Chancellor of the Exchequer, was one of the two witnesses for the prosecution. (*The Times*)

1987: White Hart Lane Football Stadium in Tottenham was the venue for a boxing match between two heavyweights, Franck Bruno, twenty-five, and Joe Bugner, thirty-seven. Bruno knocked down his opponent in the eighth round and took home £750,000. (*Sun*)

2003: On this day the Concorde made its final supersonic flight, travelling at twice the speed of sound from New York City's JFK international landing at London's Heathrow airport. It ended supersonic flight. (*Daily Mail*)

OCTOBER 25TH

1760: On this morning King George II rose as usual at 6 a.m. at Kensington Palace, drank a cup of hot chocolate and went to the toilet, alone. After a few minutes his valet heard a loud crash. He rushed into the room to find his master on the floor. He died shortly afterwards of a heart attack.

———◆———

1885: Today Mrs Broughton, a procuress, gave evidence at the Old Bailey in the case of Eliza Armstrong, a thirteen-year-old girl sold into prostitution by her hard-up mother for £5. (*Pall Mall Gazette*)

———◆———

1961: *Private Eye* was launched in London. It was initially edited by Christopher Booker as a vehicle for jokes, but became a vehicle for satire. (*Guardian*)

———◆———

1976: The National Theatre, originally suggested in 1848 and only started in 1951 when the first stone was laid, was eventually officially opened by HM the Queen on this day. The South Bank complex was still incomplete but would be finished by the end of the year. (*Guardian*)

OCTOBER 26TH

1623: A congregation of about 300 assembled in an upper room of the French ambassador's residence to hear the Jesuit Father Drury. The floor collapsed, Drury, another priest and about 100 of the congregation were killed. This was attributed to God's judgement against the Jesuits. (City of London Records Office)

————◆•————

1950: The first meeting was held in the rebuilt chamber of the House of Commons; it had been destroyed by enemy action on 10 May 1941.

————◆•————

1981: Kenneth Howarth, an explosives officer with the Metropolitan Police, was killed whilst attempting to defuse an IRA bomb in the basement toilet of a Wimpy restaurant on Oxford Street. (*Daily Mail*)

————◆•————

1998: On this Monday night, Ron Davies, MP and Welsh Secretary, was 'robbed at knifepoint' after meeting a stranger as he strolled on Clapham Common. He said he picked up a man and a woman before driving to Brixton, where the passengers turned on him and took his car, wallet and phone. He resigned as Welsh Secretary shortly afterwards. (*Evening Standard*)

OCTOBER 27TH

1899: Louise Masset, a half-French teacher of music and languages, collected her young son, Manfred, from Miss Helen Gentle of Clyde Road, Tottenham, where he was boarding. She explained that his father now wished him to be brought up in France. His naked corpse was found in a lavatory in Dalston Junction – he had been stunned and then suffocated. His mother could give no adequate explanation, but she had just broken up with a new boyfriend. She was executed in January. (*The Times*)

1986: Today the London Stock Exchange rules changed: financial markets were deregulated and fixed commission charges were abolished. This was dubbed the 'Big Bang' and increased the dominance of the City in world markets. (*Financial Times*)

1997: In thick fog the dredger mv *Sand Kite* collided with one of the Thames Barrier's piers. As the vessel started to sink, it dumped 3,300 tonnes of aggregate and then sank on top of one of the Barrier's gates. The boat was re-floated on 10 November. (*Daily Telegraph*)

OCTOBER 28TH

1215: This day was the first recorded Lord Mayor's Show, in which the Lord Mayor swears allegiance to his monarch. William Hardell, a Magna Carta signatory and City Alderman, was elected Lord Mayor of London and went in procession from the City to Westminster to swear allegiance to King John. (City of London Records Office)

1647: On this day at St Mary's church, Putney, a series of debates under the chairmanship of Lt-Gen. Oliver Cromwell started, to determine the course of England's future – a monarchy or a republic, a living King exiled or not? These debates lasted until November.

1664: 'The Duke of York and Albany's Regiment of Foot' was formed at New Artillery Grounds of Bunhill Fields on City Road. It was later to be called the Corps of HM's Royal Marines, a maritime commando infantry unit. (City of London Records Office)

1958: The State Opening of Parliament was televised for the first time, on the BBC. (BBC)

OCTOBER 29TH

1618: Sir Walter Raleigh, implicated in a plot against King James, was beheaded on this day at Old Palace Yard, Westminster. He faced death with fortitude. (City of London Records Office)

———◆———

1967: Jack McVitie, a notorious London drug dealer and hitman, was murdered by Reginald Kray at a party in Stoke Newington. Kray stabbed McVitie after his gun jammed. Kray was later found guilty of the murder in 1969 and received life imprisonment. (*Daily Mail*)

———◆———

1986: The final stretch of the M25, London Colney to South Mimms, was opened by Margaret Thatcher, the Prime Minister. The first breakdown on the completed M25 occurred at 11.16 a.m., hours after the Prime Minister had declared it open. The M25 inspired Chris Rea's hit 'Road to Hell'. (*Evening Standard*)

———◆———

2008: On this Wednesday London experienced its first October snowfall in more than seventy years. A spokesman from the Met Office said it was London's first October snow since 1934. (*Guardian*)

OCTOBER 30TH

1397: The younger son of a knightly family, Dick Whittington, who had come to London to learn a trade, became Lord Mayor of London. He was also Mayor of Calais. (City of London Records Office)

————◆◆————

1830: On this day St John Long, a 'physician', was found guilty of the manslaughter of Miss Cashin and was sentenced to pay a fine of £250. (*Newgate Calendar*)

————◆◆————

1841: A fire began in the Boyer Tower at the Tower of London. The fire then spread to the Grand Storehouse and destroyed both buildings. The Crown Jewels were almost lost because the only key was with the Lord Chamberlain – the bravery of one policeman rescued them. (City of London Records Office)

————◆◆————

1925: At his workshop at No. 22 Frith Street, Soho, above what is now Bar Italia, John Logie Baird made the first ever television transmission of a moving image – a fifteen-year-old office boy called William Tayton was paid half a crown for the privilege of being filmed!

OCTOBER 31ST

1795: John Keats (1795-1820) was born on this day and baptised at St Botolph-without-Bishopsgate on 18 December. He lived in Moorgate and became a medical student at Guy's Hospital, but abandoned his studies for writing.

———◆———

1964: The Windmill Theatre in Great Windmill Street, Soho, closed on this day for conversion to a cinema. Its slogan 'We never close' had referred to the fact that it continued its sexy shows throughout the war! Tony Hancock, Peter Sellers and Spike Milligan were some of the comedians who participated in the Windmill's Revuedeville show. (*Evening Standard*)

———◆———

1971: An IRA bomb exploded at the top of the Post Office Tower, damaging three floors. The observation floor was closed to the public. (*The Times*)

———◆———

1972: The last service at the church of St Mary-at-Lambeth in the shadow of Lambeth Palace was held on this day. It was later turned into the Museum of Garden History.

NOVEMBER 1ST

1604: The first recorded performance of *Othello* was at Whitehall Palace with Richard Burbage, the actor-manager, playing the title role. Richard Burbage, unlike Alleyn or Shakespeare, never retired from the stage, but continued to act until his death in 1619. (*Revels*)

---•◆•---

1848: The first WH Smith bookstall opened at Euston station. The company had successfully brokered an agreement with the London & North Western Railway to provide station bookstalls. (*The Times*)

---•◆•---

1946: *A Matter of Life and Death* premiered at the Empire, Leicester Square. A romantic fantasy film set in the Second World War, it was directed by Michael Powell and Emeric Pressburger, and starred David Niven and Kim Hunter. It was also chosen as the first ever Royal Film Performance, now the principal fundraiser for the Cinema and Television Benevolent Fund founded in 1924. The film was screened in the presence of King George VI, Queen Elizabeth and the Princesses Elizabeth and Margaret. (*The Times*)

NOVEMBER 2ND

1529: On this day King Henry VIII engineered the transfer of York Place from the See of York to his own possession. Whitehall Palace, as it was soon called for no conclusive reason, became the Royal home.

1824: Henry Fauntleroy, a partner of Marsh, Sibbald & Co., bankers of Berners Street, was sentenced to death for forgery. Despite attempts to have his sentence committed to life imprisonment, he was executed at Newgate before an estimated 100,000 people. (*Great Trials*)

1936: The BBC's first high definition television service was officially inaugurated with a transmission from Alexandra Palace. The programme was received by only 20,000 television-owning homes within thirty-five miles of the palace, and was described as 'flickering'. (BBC)

1953: The Samaritans, based in the crypt of St Stephen's Walbrook, received its first call on this day. It was founded by the Revd Chad Varah, vicar of St Stephen's, with the stated aim 'to befriend the suicidal and despairing'. The Samaritans received a deluge of calls after publicity in the *Daily Mirror* on 7 December. (*The Times*)

NOVEMBER 3RD

1450: On this day Jack Cade, leading about 20,000 armed men from Kent 'to punish evil ministers, and procure a redress of grievances', invaded London and beheaded the Lord Treasurer, Lord Saye.

——•••——

1783: John Austin, a highwayman, was convicted of 'Robbery with violence' on the first day of November and was hanged on this day. He was the last man hanged at Tyburn Tree. (*Newgate Calendar*)

——•••——

1949: The BBC purchased Lime Grove Studios, a film studio complex built down by the Gaumont Film Co. in Shepherds Bush, 'as a temporary measure' because they would build the Television Centre at nearby White City. They converted these studios from film to television use and reopened them on 21 May 1950. The studios were eventually sold and demolished for redevelopment in 1993. (BBC)

——•••——

1993: Twenty-seven-year-old Samantha Bissett and her four-year-old daughter Jazmine were killed in a frenzied knife attack at her flat in Plumstead – a fingerprint discovered at the flat led police to the paranoid schizophrenic Robert Napper. (*Guardian*)

NOVEMBER 4TH

1852: The House of Commons Press Gallery, where journalists are allowed to sit or gather to observe and then report speeches or events, was opened. It represents the 300 journalists accredited by the Serjeant at Arms for passes to the House of Commons.

———◆———

1890: The London Underground Tube City & South London Line between Stockwell and King William Street was the first deep-level underground electric railway in the world and took three years to build. It was opened on this day by Edward, Prince of Wales, who travelled in it from north to south. In the first year over 5 million people used the line. (London Transport Museum)

———◆———

1964: A clock, with 4ft-high mechanical figures of Mr Fortnum and Mr Mason who emerge from separate pavilions on the hour every hour, placed two floors upon the fascia of the celebrated Piccadilly store, started today. It was commissioned by Garfield Weston and designed by Berkeley Sutcliffe. (Fortnum & Mason Archives)

NOVEMBER 5TH

1605: 'A most horrible conspiracy of the Papists against the King' was discovered. The Gunpowder Plot and Guy Fawkes are remembered with fireworks to this day. The jury is still out as to whether it was a government ploy to garner public favour, which it desperately needed.

1709: Henry Sacheverell, vicar of St Saviour's Southwark, preached a sermon on this day on the 'perils of False Brethren, in Church and State' at St Paul's Cathedral, comparing the Gunpowder Plot to the execution of Charles I as 'two days of rage of both Popish and fanatical enemies of our Church and Government'. (*Daily Courant*)

1739: English journeymen weavers tried to pull down the house of a master in Spital Square, who had allegedly tried to get silk binding done free as part of the price of a weaving job. Guards were called out and several soldiers were dangerously wounded by bricks and tiles. (City of London Records Office)

1964: The Royal College of Physicians, designed by Denis Lasdun on the site of a bomb-damaged Summeries House, was opened in Regent's Park.

NOVEMBER 6TH

1429: The eight-year-old Henry VI was crowned at Westminster Abbey. His reign 'has strong claims to be considered the most calamitous in the whole of British history.'

———◆———

1838: On this day *The Times* reported a fracas on the borders of the City and Tower Hamlets which had occured the previous night when a group of Irish workers and schoolboys took umbrage at the cries of 'No Popery', attacked the bonfire boys and carried off the guy in triumph.

———◆———

1869: Queen Victoria officially opened Blackfriars Bridge over the Thames. (*The Times*)

———◆———

1963: British European Airways opened an air terminal on the Cromwell Road, some distance from the nearest underground station. (*The Times*)

———◆———

2007: The newly refurbished St Pancras station, renamed St Pancras International, launched the High Speed 1 service – the Queen and the Duke of Edinburgh were guests of honour. (*Evening Standard*)

NOVEMBER 7TH

1722: *The Conscious Lovers*, a sentimental comedy written by Richard Steele, opened on this night at the Theatre Royal, Drury Lane, and was an immediate success. It had an initial run of eighteen consecutive nights. The play was a departure from the normal lewd comedies and relied on the comedy involved keeping a social morality, as well as restrained passions and patience.

————◆◆————

1729: On this day *Bradley's Weekly Messenger* reported that a fire extinguisher, patented by Ambrose Godfrey Hauckwitz, was used to great effect to put out a fire in the city.

————◆◆————

1841: Field Lane School, Saffron Hill, was opened today for forty-five boys and girls, by Andrew Provan. It was one of the most famous 'Ragged' Schools, established to teach and feed the London underclasses. (*The Times*)

————◆◆————

1863: S.H. Hunt, a servant of Butler and McCulloch's seedsmen, Covent Garden, poisoned his wife and children in a cab, and himself two days later, at his own house, just before his apprehension. (*Daily Telegraph*)

NOVEMBER 8TH

1674: The poet John Milton died 'of gout' on this day. He was buried in St Giles-without-Cripplegate.

———◆———

1924: The Fortune Theatre in Russell Street opened. It was the first West End theatre to be rebuilt after the war, and has an underground passageway into the Crown Court Scottish church. (*The Times*)

———◆———

1974: In the early hours, Richard J. Bingham, seventh Earl of Lucan, disappeared, following the killing of Sandra Rivett, his children's nanny, the previous evening. He was presumed dead in 1992 and declared officially dead in 1999. This unresolved crime continues to fascinate. Speculations are that Lord Lucan may still be alive and living in a remote corner of the globe. Inconsistencies in the evidence have even led journalists to believe that enough doubt could be raised to acquit Lord Lucan of murder. (*Daily Telegraph*)

———◆———

1974: The Covent Garden fruit and vegetable market closed, reopening three days later at the 68-acre Nine Elms site. (*Daily Mail*)

NOVEMBER 9TH

1462: Southwark Fair, already long established, was Chartered on this day. (City of London Records Office)

———◆———

1783: The first public hanging outside Newgate Prison took place on this day when ten criminals were hanged with the 'new drop' system, by Edward Dennis. Edward Dennis, the hangman, was no saint either. He had been imprisoned in Newgate in 1780 and sentenced to death for taking part in the Holborn riots. He was later reprieved so he could hang his fellow rioters. (*Newgate Calendar*)

———◆———

1922: The mentally ill Walter Tatam sent the very unpopular Assistant Commissioner Francis Horwood a box of chocolates (Walnut Whips) laced with arsenic. Assuming they were a birthday present from his daughter, the Assistant Commissioner ate one and only survived because of the prompt attention of the police surgeons. Disliked for his lack of social graces, he was then contemptuously nicknamed the 'Chocolate Soldier'. (*The Times*)

———◆———

1947: Telerecording was used for the first time when the Remembrance Service from the Cenotaph in London was filmed by the BBC and recorded for transmission that evening. (BBC)

NOVEMBER 10TH

1558: Elizabeth I, Queen of England, came to the throne on this day after the death of her half-sister, Queen Mary, who died without heirs.

———◆———

1668: Queen Elizabeth's Day, a day created to celebrate the return to Protestantism, was first celebrated on this day, and continued every year with increasing fervour. (City of London Records Office)

———◆———

1913: John Richard Archer (1863-1932), a photographer, son of Richard, a black ship's steward, and Mary Burns, of Ireland, was elected Mayor of Battersea by thirty votes to twenty-nine, by the Progressive Party. He was the first mixed-race man to be a mayor in London. (*Daily Mail*)

———◆———

1924: The BBC transmitted for the first time, running commentary on an outside broadcast from the Lord Mayor's Show.

———◆———

1929: The thirteen-year-old Yehudi Menuhin gave his first public performance at the Royal Albert Hall. (*The Times*)

November 11th

1737: Mary Young was imprisoned in Bridewell in the City for 'raising great disturbances in the Hanging Sword Alley, Fleet Street with other loose, idle and disorderly persons and common street walkers'. (*Newgate Calendar*)

1920: The bodies of two unknown First World War soldiers were buried, one in Westminster Abbey, and one beneath the Arc de Triomphe in Paris. (*The Times*)

1920: The Cenotaph was unveiled by King George V in Whitehall. (*Daily Mail*)

1983: On this day Mary Donaldson (1921-2003) became the first woman to be Lord Mayor of the City of London. (*The Times*)

1999: The Greater London Authority Act received Royal Assent on this day. It was the first Act that established the London Assembly and the Mayor of London. It was brought in after a referendum which resulted in a 'Yes' vote. It also created a Metropolitan Police Authority.

NOVEMBER 12TH

1688: The building of smart streets around St James's Square prompted better lighting; St James's churchyard was 'lit by the lights as are used in Jermine Street'. (Central London Records Office)

1919: This day saw the first flight from Britain to Australia. Ross Macpherson Smith and brother Keith, and Sergeants Jim Bennett and Wally Shiers flew from Hounslow Heath in a Vickers Vimy, eventually landing in Darwin, Australia on 10 December, taking less than twenty-eight days, with an actual flying time of 135 hours. (*Australian Dictionary of Biography*)

1974: The first salmon to be caught in the Thames in fifty years was caught in an in-take screen at a power station, but the Water Authority decided it did not count as it was not landed by a fisherman and it was not a Thames salmon – just misguided! The Silver Cup went to an angler, Russell Doig, on 3 September 1983, when he caught a 2kg salmon upriver in Chertsey. Cheekily he took a photograph of himself and his catch with Tower Bridge behind them. (*Evening Standard*)

NOVEMBER 13TH

1849: Frederick and Maria Manning were hanged in front of a crowd of 50,000, which included Charles Dickens, for the murder of Maria's lover, Patrick O'Connor. This was the first 'media' hanging. The verdict was also greatly influenced by the press. (*The Times*)

1887: 'Bloody Sunday', an Irish nationalist and a socialist rally in Trafalgar Square, turned into a full-scale riot in which two protestors wre killed and and many more were beaten by the police. (*The Times*)

1895: On his way from the London Court to Reading Gaol, Oscar Wilde stood on Clapham Junction platform in convict dress, handcuffed between two policemen; 'Of all possible objects I was the most grotesque. Each train as it swelled the audience. Nothing could exceed their amusement. For half an hour I stood there in the grey November rain surrounded by a jeering mob.' (*De Profundis*)

1920: Clashes took place between police and demonstrators in Trafalgar Square at a meeting called to protest against a ban on open-air meetings and to call for the release of an Irish MP who had been supporting a rent strike. Two demonstrators were killed. (*The Times*)

NOVEMBER 14TH

1635: On this day 'Old Parr' died. Supposedly born around 1483, Thomas Parr had married at the age of eighty and had two children who died young. He remarried when 122. He was brought to London by the Earl of Arundel, but died shortly afterwards and was buried in Westminster Abbey. (City of London Records Office)

———•◆•———

1864: Franz Muller was convicted of the first railway murder, that of Thomas Briggs, a bank clerk found badly injured on the railway line between Hackney Wick and Bow. He was hanged on this day outside Newgate. 'He died before such a concourse as we hope may never be again assembled.' (*The Times*)

———•◆•———

1896: The 'Emancipation Run', later known as the 'London to Brighton Car Rally', took place to celebrate the increase in the speed limit from 4 to 14mph. (*The Times*)

———•◆•———

1935: In the General Election the seat of Westminster St George's was contested by two cousins: Alfred Duff-Cooper for the Conservatives and Mrs Anne Fremantle for Labour. Mr Duff-Cooper won with a majority of 20,000.

NOVEMBER 15TH

1635: On this day the Archbishop of Canterbury, William Laud, recorded that, 'at afternoon the greatest Tide that hath been seen. It came within my gates, walks, cloysters and stables at Lambeth'.

———◆———

1712: On this day in Hyde Park, early in the morning, James, Duke of Hamilton, and Charles, Lord Mohun, fought a sword duel over a claim on the Macclesfield Estate by the Duke. George MacCartney, Mohun's second, killed Hamilton, and Mohun died of his wounds shortly after. Largely as a result of the horrific injuries sustained by the parties, the government brought in legislation banning the use of seconds. (*London Journal*)

———◆———

1979: On this day Margaret Thatcher, the Prime Minister, named Sir Anthony Blunt, a former security service officer and Personal Adviser on Art to the Queen, as the 'fourth man' in the Philby affair. He had been recruited by Russia in the 1930s and was a close friend of Guy Burgess. He was stripped of his knighthood. (*The Times*)

NOVEMBER 16TH

1724: Jack Sheppard, the diminutive thief and working-class hero, was taken from Newgate to Tyburn to be hanged. His hanging was attended by a crowd of 200,000, and he was buried in the churchyard of St Martin-in-the-Fields that evening. He was only twenty-two. (*Newgate Calendar*)

1898: On this Wednesday Britain's first escalator was installed in Harrods. Customers were so overcome that attendants were posted at the top to administer brandy to gentlemen and smelling salts to the ladies! (*The Times*)

London Underground's first escalator was at Earl's Court in 1911. 'Bumper' Harris, who had a wooden leg, was employed to travel up and down on the 'moving staircase' to show how easy it was to use. (*The Times*)

1996: Southwark Cathedral became a focus of controversy by hosting a twentieth anniversary for the Lesbian and Gay Christian Movement. (*Daily Mail*)

November 17th

1558: On this day probably the most unpopular British monarch, the Catholic Queen Mary, the only surviving child of Henry VIII and Catherine of Aragon, died at St James's Palace, London.

———◆◆———

1750: 'Earth hath not anything to show more fair' – at midnight the long-awaited Westminster Bridge opened to the sound of drums, cannons and trumpets, for foot passengers and horses. Designed by a Swiss, Charles Labelye, the bridge had fourteen arches and the parapet had alcoves. (*London Journal*)

———◆◆———

2011: During the Bruckner Concert performed by the London Philharmonic Orchestra at the South Bank, a tall man left the choir section and walked to the exit, shouting 'terrible'. According to members of the audience, he managed to completely break the spell of the performance. The perpetrator of the disturbance later wrote to *Slipped Disc*. His retort was that the performance was lacklustre, amateur and very badly rehearsed. He had in fact said '… It's far too slow … Why aren't you more critical? It's rubbish'. (*Arts Journal*)

NOVEMBER 18TH

1750: On this Saturday Westminster Bridge opened – 'All next day Westminster was like a fair … 32 lamps were fixed up and 12 watchmen appointed to do duty every night …' (*London Journal*)

———•———

1910: Black Friday – on this day 300 suffragettes clashed violently with the police at a rally in Hyde Park. Their protest was in response to Prime Minister Herbert Asquith's refusal to allow more parliamentary time for reading the Conciliation Bill – a bill that would extend the rights of women to vote. It was the first documented use of force against women; two women died and 200 were arrested. (*The Times*)

———•———

1987: On this day a discarded cigarette or match ignited debris beneath the wooden escalators at Kings Cross St Pancras station. A large fire combined with toxic fumes killed thirty-one. Almost all wooden escalators on the network have now been replaced with steel ones. (*The Times*)

November 19th

1795: Richard Brothers, a believer and preacher of Anglo-Israelism, claiming that the Anglo-Saxons were one of the lost tribes of Israel and placed in a private asylum for the originally insane in Islington, proclaimed that on this day he would be revealed as Prince of the Hebrews and Ruler of the World. (*Morning Post*)

1947: King George VI created Philip Mountbatten Duke of Edinburgh, in preparation for his marriage to Princess Elizabeth the next day.

1987: A 1931 Bugatti Royale was sold at a Christie's auction at the Royal Albert Hall for £5.5 million to Swedish property tycoon Hans Thulin. (*The Times*)

1994: Britain's first lottery draw was aired live in London. A £1 ticket gave the gambler a 1-in-14-million chance of striking lucky and guessing correctly the winning six out of forty-nine numbers. The lottery operator, Camelot, said about 15 million players had purchased 35 million tickets from retailers – seven jackpot winners each won £800,000 in the draw. (*Daily Mail*)

November 20th

1572: On this day a presbytery for dissenters was established in Wandsworth. (Wandsworth Archives)

—◆—

1902: A group of University College students, led by William Lister, crossed the Thames to Battersea with a crowbar and sledgehammer to attack the statue of the 'Brown Dog' on the Latchmere Estate, put there in 1906 to commemorate animal cruelty. The students were discovered trying to dismantle the statue. Ten were arrested by two police officers, the rioting escalated and further incursions were made into Battersea, turning what had been a difference of opinion into a class war. (*Daily Graphic*)

—◆—

1944: After five years of blackout, Piccadilly Circus and the Strand's lights were switched on again. (*Daily Mail*)

—◆—

2002: The UK's first public autopsy for 170 years was performed by Professor Gunther von Hagens in front of a sell-out crowd of 500 people in the Atlantis Gallery in Spitalfields, despite the police advising that they might prosecute him. (*Guardian*)

NOVEMBER 21ST

1846: On this day the first appearance in print of 'Sweeney Todd' was in the Penny Dreadful *The String of Pearls* – there is no evidence that he really existed.

1872: Two young Prussians, Herman Nagel and Paul May, came to London to avoid conscription. Once their money ran out they agreed to commit suicide – after wounding May, Nagel killed himself on 21 August. May recovered, was indicted for murder and was on this day acquitted. (*The Times*)

1953: The Natural History Museum announced that the Piltdown Man skull, initially thought to be one of the most important archaeological finds, was a fake. (*Daily Telegraph*)

1989: The proceedings of the House of Commons were televised for the first time. (*The Times*)

2011: The Attorney General, the *Guardian* reported on this day, would be applying for permission to bring Contempt of Court Proceedings against the *Daily Mail* and the *Mirror* over their 'prejudicial' reporting of the conviction of Levi Bellfield for the murder of Milly Dowler.

NOVEMBER 22ND

1774: General Robert Clive (1725-1774), Baron Clive of Plassey, a contentious figure in the governance of India, died of 'an excessively large dose of opium at his house in Berkeley Square'. (*Oxford Dictionary of National Biography*)

———•◆•———

1819: Thirty-two pigeons were let loose at 7 a.m. in London. The first arrived in Antwerp at midday, the second a quarter of an hour later. The rest followed the next day. (*The Times*)

———•◆•———

1860: East End costermongers (sellers of fruit and vegetables) held a meeting to state their grievances against the police who restricted their livelihood. The Metropolitan Streets Act was modified accordingly. (*The Times*)

———•◆•———

1873: Sir David Salomons died on this day. He was a leading figure in Jewish emancipation, becoming the first Jewish magistrate, the first Jewish Sheriff of the City of London and in 1855 the first Jewish Lord Mayor of London. (*The Times*)

———•◆•———

1990: Margaret Thatcher was forced to stand down as Prime Minister. Twenty-four hours earlier she had won the first round of elections for her party, but the Cabinet refused to back her in the second round. (*Daily Telegraph*)

NOVEMBER 23RD

1499: The Flemish impostor claiming to be Richard, Duke of York, but who was in fact Perkin Warbeck, was executed in London. He had caused evil unrest and rebellion. (City of London Records Office)

———◆———

1858: The Medical Act 1858 was to create a body now known as the General Medical Council but then known as the General Council of Medical Education and Registration. It held its first meeting in London on this day.

———◆———

1887: William Henry Pratt, better known as Boris Karloff, the actor, was born at No. 36 Forest Hill Road. His great-aunt's story of life in the Royal Court of Siam formed the basis of *The King and I*. (Authors archives)

———◆———

2006: Alexander Litvinenko, a Russian dissident and former member of the Russian Security Police, the FSB, died at University College Hospital under suspicious circumstances. His death was later attributed to poisoning with radioactive polonium-210. A posthumous statement accused Vladimir Putin of arranging his death. (*Daily Telegraph*)

NOVEMBER 24TH

1434: On this day a severe frost began and continued until 10 February the following year. The Thames froze over. (City of London Records Office)

———— • ◆ • ————

1740: William Duell was hanged at Tyburn. He was prepared for dissection by surgeons, only to breathe again. He was then deported. (*Newgate Calendar*)

———— • ◆ • ————

1997: The new British Library Humanities Reading Room, adjacent to the Midland Grand Hotel, was opened. One observer remarked that it 'offered no pomposity, no sentimentality and above all no dripping English nostalgia', a view shared by the Price of Wales. (*Guardian*)

———— • ◆ • ————

2011: Piccadilly's forty-eight-year-old one-way system was opened to two-way traffic in an attempt by Westminster Council and Transport for London to ease congestion. It was part of a £14 million project which in July began letting traffic drive in both directions along Pall Mall and St James's Street. The revamp also included new footpaths and lighting. (*London Evening Standard*)

NOVEMBER 25TH

1703: A huge windstorm swept over southern England. In London the lead roofing was blown off Westminster Abbey, and Queen Anne had to shelter in a cellar in St James's Palace to avoid falling chimneys and masonry. The storm was generally reckoned to be a result of the the anger of God because of the 'Crying Sins of the Nation'. (*British Journal for the History of Science*)

———•◆•———

1929: The Duchess Theatre in Catherine Street opened, but became a cinema within three years. This Mock Tudor building was designed by architect Ewan Barr.

———•◆•———

1944: By this date, 251 V2 bombs had dropped on London.

———•◆•———

1952: A murder mystery play, *The Mousetrap* by Agatha Christie, opened at the New Ambassadors Theatre and ran at this theatre until 1974, when it transferred to the St Martin's Theatre. It is still going, having notched up over 24,500 performances. (*Daily Mail*)

NOVEMBER 26TH

1703: At about 11 p.m. a hurricane struck London. It rolled the lead sheets off the roofs, destroyed spires and turrets, and drove ships from London Bridge to Limehouse. (*History of London*, Henry Chamberlain)

1962: The Beatles recorded 'Please Please Me' at the Abbey Road Studios. George Martin had originally thought an earlier version dreary and considered releasing another song instead, but the version the 'Fab Four' came up with on this day was a potential hit! (*The Beatles*, 2000)

1969: In an interview at her London home, Margaret Thatcher said, 'No woman in my time will be Prime Minister or Chancellor of the Exchequer or Foreign Secretary – not the top jobs. Anyway, I would not want to be Prime Minister, you have to give yourself 100 per cent'. (*Sunday Telegraph*)

1983: Gold bars worth £26 million were stolen from the Brink's-Mat security warehouse at Heathrow Airport. It was Britain's biggest robbery of the time. The investigation took nearly ten years and a large percentage of the bullion was never found. (*Evening Standard*)

NOVEMBER 27TH

1810: Mrs Tottenham of No. 54 Berners Street was visited by coal merchants, upholsterers, organ makers, linen drapers and jewellers, as well as the Lord Mayor of London and Peers of the Realm. All of these had been summoned at a specific time. The normally quiet street overflowed with crowds all day to the astonishment of Mrs Tottenham! It appeared that 4,000 letters had been received by those visiting. It was obviously a hoax, later discovered to have been perpetrated by the wit Theodore Hook. (*Dictionary of National Biography*)

1955: On this Sunday, the Battersea funfair in Battersea Park opened for the first time on a Sunday, although a petition of protest was signed by 15,000 people.

2000: The ten-year old schoolboy Damilola Taylor was brutally attacked and 'shanked' (a broken bottle or knife severing the femoral artery in the thigh) by Ricky and Danny Preddie on a North Peckham estate. He bled to death and his assailants were eventually caught and sentenced to eight years' youth custody. (*Daily Express*)

NOVEMBER 28TH

1660: At Gresham College, twelve men including Christopher Wren, Robert Boyle, John Wilkins and Sir Robert Moray set up a committee for the promotion of Physico-Mathematical experimental learning. It was granted a Charter by King Charles II in 1662 as the 'Royal Society of London'. It acts as a scientific adviser to the government and as the country's Academy of Sciences, and funds research fellowships and start-up companies. It is probably the oldest such society in the world. (*London Gazette*)

————•◆•————

1757: William Blake was born at what is now Broadwick Street, Soho. He was the third of seven children, born to a dissenting couple. Although largely unrecognised during his lifetime, he became, especially through his vivid poetry, accompanied by equally vivid drawings, one of the most influential and mystical personalities of his age. (*Dictionary of National Biography*)

————•◆•————

1919: The American Nancy Astor, married to the anglicised Waldorf, 2nd Viscount Astor, became the first woman to be elected (and take her seat) in the House of Commons. She took her seat on 1 December. (*The Times*)

NOVEMBER 29TH

1814: On this day *The Times* was printed by steam instead of manual power. It was the first newspaper ever to be printed in this way. The steam printing press was invented by the German printer Friedrich König, and was capable of printing 1,100 sheets an hour.

1855: A public meeting was held at Willis's Rooms to raise funds to establish an institution for the training of nurses and other hospital attendants. This was the start of the Nightingale Fund and would create the Nightingale School of Nursing. (Royal College of Nursing Archives)

1934: Prince George, Duke of Kent, fifth child of George V and Mary of Teck, married Princess Marina of Greece at Westminster Abbey. Her bridesmaids were Princesses Irene, Eugenie and Katherine of Greece, the Grand Duchess Kirilovna of Russia, and Crown Princess Juliana of the Netherlands. The Royal School of Needlework made a quilt as a wedding present. (*The Times*)

NOVEMBER 30TH

1016: King Edmund II of England (*c.* 988/993-1016) was reputedly stabbed in the bowels whilst in the 'outhouse' (toilet) and died, in London, on the same day.

1936: A small fire in a lavatory in the central transept of the Crystal Palace at Sydenham turned into a conflagration and destroyed the whole building. The red glow of the fire could be seen from Brighton. In spite of the eighty-eight fire engines sent from the four Fire Brigades deployed to fight the fire, by dawn the building was completely devastated. Melted glass lay everywhere, girders partly melted by the intensity of the blaze. The only elements left unscathed were Paxton's bust and some sphinxes. Because of lack of funds, the palace was not fully insured and rebuilding was out of the question. Winston Churchill saw the blaze and uttered the prescient words, 'This is the end of an age'. It had been beset by bad luck; the Palace was damaged by strong winds in 1861, and in 1866 a fire had destroyed the north end of the building. (BBC)

DECEMBER 1ST

1582: Thomas Campion, a Jesuit priest who had secretly come to England to encourage Roman Catholics, was caught, tried, and hanged, drawn and quartered at Tyburn on this Thursday. (City of London Records Office)

1652: The Act of Parliament which ordered the sale of Crown Lands after the execution of Charles I excepted Hyde Park from its provisions – but on this day it became the subject of a special resolution, 'That Hyde Park be sold for ready money'. It was about sixty-two acres and sold for £17,066 2s 8d. (*Victoria County Histories*)

1683: From this day until 5 February 1684, the weather was so cold that the Thames froze over. Shops were erected on the ice and a Frost Fair was held. (*John Evelyn's Diary*)

1967: Pipaluk the polar bear cub was born to Sam and Sally at the London Zoo. He left for Poland in 1985 when the terraces that housed all the bears were closed. (*The Times*)

DECEMBER 2ND

1697: The first service was held on this day in Sir Christopher Wren's new cathedral, St Paul's, although the final stone was not laid until 1710. It is the second largest church in Britain, after Liverpool Cathedral. (City of London Records Office)

1887: On this day *A Study in Scarlet* was first published as a book by Ward Locke, establishing No. 221B Baker Street as the home of Mr Sherlock Holmes, Britain's first 'serial' detective. (*Birmingham Daily Post*)

1718: A shop signboard hanging in Fleet Street, opposite Bridge Lane, became loosened by recent winds. This in turn loosed the brickwork, which gave way and fell, bringing the house down and killing four people, including the Queen's Jeweller. (*London Gazette*)

2009: 'Lord' Edward Davenport of Portland Place was jailed for seven years and eight months for conning fifty-one victims. The self-styled aristocrat and entrepreneur cashed in on the credit crunch by offering bogus loans for cash-strapped investors. He pocketed millions of pounds in deposits and advance fees and never paid out the loans. (*Daily Mail*)

DECEMBER 3RD

1754: Tobias Smollett lost his watch and money when his stagecoach was held up between Chelsea and London. (City of London Records Office)

1930: The fourth Adelphi Theatre in the Strand opened. It was designed by Ernest Schauffenberg 'with a complete absence of curves'. (*The Times*)

1954: The premiere of the opera *Troilus and Cressida* by William Walton was held at the Royal Opera House, Covent Garden. (*Daily Mail*)

1976: A giant inflatable pig, nicknamed Algie, broke free from its moorings. It was being photographed for the forthcoming Pink Floyd 'Animals' album cover. The Civil Aviation Authority issued a warning to all pilots that a flying pig was on the run. (*Evening Standard*)

1976: An estimated 3 million people applied for Abba's Albert Hall concerts – there were just over 11,000 tickets available. (*Daily Mail*)

1993: Princess Diana, in the throes of a separation and eventual divorce, issued a statement that she would be withdrawing from public life because media intrusion was detrimental. (*The Times*)

DECEMBER 4TH

1791: The first edition of the Sunday newspaper the *Observer* appeared and was given out free. W.S. Bourne, its founder, proclaimed its commitment to reporting news and 'The Fine Arts, emanation of Sciences Tragi-Comedy, national policies and fashion'. It remains the oldest Sunday newspaper still published.

This first edition of the *Observer* mentioned that 'a West-country gentleman, not much acquainted with the ways of London, expressed great surprise a few nights ago at the "flocks" of "chicken prostitutes" before Somerset House and which he actually mistook for the pupils of some large boarding school. One of the young "Misses", however, soon convinced him of his error by granting a favour, which will probably retard his journey home for some time'.

———◆———

1947: A Christmas ceremony has occurred every first Thursday of December since this year. A Norway spruce or fir is given by Norway's capital Oslo, and presented as London's Christmas tree as a token of gratitude for Britain's support during the Second World War. The tree is lit on this day and taken down just before twelfth night.

DECEMBER 5TH

1660: On this Wednesday the Parliamentary Committee for the Post Office resolved that the Postmaster General be spoken to about the rates of foreign letters and should endeavour to reduce them to certain and fit rates. (*Journal of the House of Commons*)

1766: James Christie (1730-1803) held his first auction sale in London on this day.

1905: Henry Campbell-Bannerman, the Liberal leader, became the First Lord of the Treasury to be officially called 'Prime Minister'.

1952: A layer of dense fog created by a sharp cold, lack of wind and a combination of industrial and domestic smoke, engulfed London for four days. This resulted in the death of upwards of 12,000 people and the eventual Clean Air Act of 1956.

1991: Following the death of Robert Maxwell in the Mediterranean, administrators were called in on this day to try to salvage his Empire – this included the Mirror Group. (*Daily Telegraph*)

DECEMBER 6TH

1648: The parliamentarian Col. Thomas Pride expelled over 100 Presbyterian Royalist MPs in what became known as 'Pride's Purge'. The House, reduced to eighty members, later started proceedings against King Charles I.

———•◆•———

1917: A huge German air raid attacked Chelsea, Brixton, Battersea, Stepney, Whitechapel, Clerkenwell and Shoreditch.

———•◆•———

1964: The Rev. Martin Luther King, the black American Civil Rights leader, gave a sermon to 4,000 people at St Paul's Cathedral. (*Daily Mail*)

———•◆•———

1975: Four IRA gunmen were pursued through the West End on this day as they had fired gunshots into Scotts Restaurant in Mount Street. They ended up holing themselves up in No. 22B Balcombe Street, Marylebone, the home of the elderly Mr and Mrs Matthews. They demanded that they and the elderly couple be flown to Ireland, but the police refused. On 12 December they capitulated. The siege and its result were watched on television by millions worldwide. (BBC)

DECEMBER 7TH

1732: The first production at the first Covent Garden Theatre opened– it was Congreve's *The Way of the World*. The best seats were actually on the stage. (*Daily Courant*)

1907: On this day the National Sporting Club, No. 43 King Street, Covent Garden, witnessed a first: at the Tommy Burns and Gunner Moir fight, Eugene Corri became the first referee to adjudicate 'inside' a boxing ring. (*Daily Mail*)

1916: David Lloyd George became Prime Minister of a coalition government after Asquith's resignation.

2006: At 11 a.m. Chamberlayne Road and surrounding streets in Kensal Green were hit by heavy rain and sleet, and then debris flying through the air. A tornado had struck. Over 150 houses were damaged and six people were injured, one of them being hospitalised. Fire services sealed off the area. The clean-up operation and damage costs were in excess of £2 million. (*Daily Mail*)

DECEMBER 8TH

1660: The oldest extant cheque in the Bank of England Museum was for £200. It was drawn on Clayton & Morris of Cornhill, written by Nicholas van Acker, and was payable to Mr Delboe.

———◆———

1660: Margaret Hughes became the first woman to appear on stage in England. She played 'Desdemona' in the *Moor of Venice* at the Vere Street Theatre in London. An accomplished manager, she would form the Theatre Court and produce a daughter by Prince Rupert.

———◆———

1762: Two Highland officers came to watch Isaac Bickerstaff's new comic opera *Love in a Village* at Covent Garden. The mob in the upper gallery shouted, 'No Scots! No Scots! Out with them!' The mob hissed and pelted them with apples. (*Boswell's London Journal*)

———◆———

1995: Philip Lawrence, aged forty-eight, the headmaster of St George's Roman Catholic School in Maida Vale, saw a group of youths attacking one of his pupils. He went out to stop it, but fifteen-year-old Learco Chindamo punched and then stabbed him. Philip Lawrence died that evening. Chindamo was convicted of the murder in October 1996. (*Evening Standard*)

DECEMBER 9TH

1621: The Fortune Theatre, Golding Lane, Cripplegate, built for Edward Alleyn and Philip Henslowe in 1600 following their success and profits made from the Rose Theatre, burnt down in two hours on this night. It was rebuilt the same year using brick – the first theatre to do so. (City of London Records Office)

———◆———

1868: William Ewart Gladstone became Prime Minister for the first time. He would become Prime Minister three more times.

———◆———

1914: Lt Harry Colebourn of the Second Canadian Infantry Brigade purchased a black bear cub in Ontario, called it Winnie after Winnipeg, brought it to England and left it at London Zoo. A.A. Milne visited the zoo as a child and based the character 'Winnie the Pooh' on it. (*The Man Who Drew Pooh*, Arthur R. Chandler)

———◆———

2011: A hypothermic ring-tailed lemur nicknamed 'King Julien' by the Blue Cross Animal Hospital in Victoria was found on this day on Tooting Common, 6,000 miles from its Madagascan home. (*Daily Mail* and *Sun*)

December 10th

1610: John Roberts, Roman Catholic priest and first Prior of St Gregory's Douai (now Downside Abbey), was arrested on 2 December. He was tried and found guilty under the Act for bidding Roman Catholic priests to minister in England, and was hanged, drawn and quartered on this day at Tyburn – his finger bone is kept at Tyburn Convent.

———◆◆———

1845: Robert Thompson, a civil engineer, patented a pneumatic tyre in London on this day. Unfortunately the process was not mechanised, therefore painfully slow to manufacture. It did not catch on until Dunlop mechanised the process. (Patent Office)

———◆◆———

1868: The first 'traffic lights', semaphore arms on either side of a metal post, which were invented by John Peake Knight, were installed on the corner of Bridge Street and New Palace Yard, by Westminster. (London Blue Plaques)

———◆◆———

1971: Frank Zappa was hurled from the stage at the Rainbow Theatre in Finsbury Park by a fan. He fell 10ft into the concrete-lined orchestra pit – the damage was such that he walked with a pronounced limp for the rest of his life. (*Guardian*)

DECEMBER 11TH

1756: On this day, a few days after leaving debtor's gaol, Theodor 'Baron von Neuhoff', King of Corsica, died in penury in a tailor's house in Little Chapel Street, Soho, and was buried in the churchyard of St Anne's. Horace Walpole composed and paid for a monumental inscription. (*Victoria County Histories*)

1769: On this day Edward Beran of London patented what became known as 'Venetian blinds'. Although they were first known before 1700 in Japan, Beran was the first to patent such a blind. (UK Intellectual Property Office)

1936: On this evening Edward VIII gave a radio address from Buckingham Palace in which he explained, 'I have found it impossible to carry out the heavy burden of responsibility and to discharge the duties of King as I would wish to do without the help and support of the woman I love'. (BBC)

1987: Charlie Chaplin's cane and bowler hat, used in his most iconic films, were sold at Christie's in London for £82,500. His boots were sold for £38,500. (*Daily Telegraph*)

DECEMBER 12TH

1688: A scrivener drinking in a public house in Wapping recognised a man dressed as a sailor as the judge he had once appeared before – Judge Jeffreys! Known as the 'hanging judge', he escaped execution but died in the Tower of London a few months later. (Lord Macaulay)

1896: Gugliemo Marconi, the Italian physicist and inventor, first publicly demonstrated his radio at Toynbee Hall in the East End. (*The Times*)

1898: Fulham, London's oldest professional football club, was granted professional status. (Football Association)

1988: Three commuter trains crashed 800m from Clapham Junction. One train stopped due to a signal malfunction, only to have another crash into it. A third train from the opposite direction ploughed into the wreckage. Thirty-five people died and 500 were injured. (*South London Press*)

1988: The first satellite pictures were beamed to over 2,000 London betting shops to enable them to watch races live from many racecourses. (*Sun*)

DECEMBER 13TH

1779: The first Smithfield Show organised by the Smithfield Cattle & Sheep Society was held at Wooton's Dolphin Yard on this day.

1867: Clerkenwell Prison's exercise yard was the target of a gunpowder explosion instigated by members of the Fenians. The blast killed bystanders in Corporation Row – some of the Fenians were later executed. (*The Times*)

1878: The Holborn Viaduct was illuminated with electricity this evening. It was installed by a French contractor who had lit a street in Lyon in 1857. (*Evening Standard*)

1904: On this day the London Underground went electric. (London Underground)

1951: Denis Thatcher married Margaret Roberts at Wesley's chapel in City Road. The reason they chose this venue was because he was divorced and her family were Methodists. (Marriage Registers)

1995: After the death of a black man, Wayne Douglas, in police custody, several hundred people converged on Brixton police station on this day. Twenty-two people were arrested and two policemen were hurt. (*South London Press*)

DECEMBER 14TH

1911: Eleanor Davies-Colley became the first woman to become a fellow of the Royal College of Surgeons in Lincolns Inn Fields. She was also a founding member of the Women's Federation and a founder of the South London Hospital for Women in Clapham. (*Oxford Dictionary of National Biography*)

1920: An aeroplane carrying six passengers and two crew members took off from Cricklewood Airport for Paris and crashed into a house in Golders Green. Of the eight on board, only two survived. This was the first scheduled flight disaster. (*Daily Mail*)

1934: Western Avenue was formally opened – it was designed to take pressure off the old Uxbridge Road and to open up the industrial estates to the west of London. (*The Times*)

2011: A chemist of the Abbey Pharmacy in Merton was taken to St George's Hospital with burns to his hand and face after staff at the pharmacy tried to get rid of a dead rat's smell by lighting a scented candle and spraying air fresheners. The store exploded and the hapless pharmacist was hurled through the front of the shop. (*South London Press*)

DECEMBER 15TH

1720: On this day John Potter, a carpenter, advertised that, 'At the New Theatre in the Haymarket, between Suffolk Street and James Street, which is now completely finished, will be acted French Comedies, as soon as the actors arrive from Paris ....'. A fortnight later the curtain rose on a production of *La Fille a La Mode*.

--- ◆ ---

1906: The Great Northern, Piccadilly & Brompton Railway, later known as the Piccadilly Tube Line, opened between Hammersmith and Finsbury Park. (*Daily Mail*)

--- ◆ ---

1927: The Church of England, being an established Church, needed approval from Parliament for any substantial changes to its *Common Book of Prayer*. On this day Parliament rejected a proposed *New Book of Common Prayer* because it 'leaned too far towards Rome' and so it was returned for further revision. As a result the shorter *Prayer Book* was the next attempt at modernisation. (Hansard)

DECEMBER 16TH

1868: At Ashley House, the London home of Lord Lindsay, Lindsay Lord Adare and Capt. Charles Wynne watched the medium and psychic Daniel 'Douglas' Home slump into a chair and go into a trance. He walked out of the room, into another, raised a window and stood on air three storeys above ground! He then repeated the exercise from another room's window. (*Psychic Journal*)

1897: William Terriss (William Charles James Lewin), an actor and heartthrob of the day, was murdered outside the Adelphi Theatre by another actor, Richard Prince. (*The Times*)

1937: The premiere of *Me and My Girl* with music by Noel Coward was at the Victoria Palace Theatre, starring Lupino Lane. It featured 'The Lambeth Walk' and a performance was televised from the theatre in 1939. (*Daily Mail*)

1977: The underground extension to Heathrow airport was opened by the Queen. London thus became the first capital in the world with a direct rail link to its airport. (*Daily Mail*)

DECEMBER 17TH

1540: The Abbey church of St Peter, Westminster, became a cathedral with its own See on this day. Ten years later it was incorporated into the diocese of London and much of its estate was sold to repair St Paul's Cathedral – hence the saying 'Robbing St Peter to pay St Paul'. (Stow)

1849: On this day James Lock & Co., Hatters of St James's Street, sold the first bowler hat, designed by hat-makers Thomas & Bowler, to the specifications of a Mr Coke, who wanted a more appropriate headgear for gamekeepers. (*The Times*)

1932: Ex-King Manuel of Portugal died on this day at Fulwell Park, Twickenham. His requiem mass was at Westminster Cathedral and his body was borne through the streets of Twickenham with the children of St Catherine's and St James's schools lining the streets. (*The Times*)

1983: An IRA bomb exploded outside Harrods, killing six and injuring ninety. One of the fatalities was twenty-two-year-old WPC Jane Arbuthnot. The car containing the bomb was projected onto the fifth floor of an adjoining building. (*Evening Standard*)

DECEMBER 18TH

1679: Late on this night, the poet John Dryden, whose works define the age in which he lived, was brutally beaten in an attack by three men in Rose Street, Covent Garden. Lord Rochester might have had a hand in hiring his assailants. Rochester had lampooned Dryden earlier, and had in turn suspected Dryden of complicity in ridiculing him in an 'Essay on Satire'. The culprits were never caught. (*Oxford Dictionary of National Biography*)

1778: Joseph Grimaldi was born in Clare Market, W1, an area between the Strand and Drury Lane. He was to become an actor and comedian, most notably 'Joey the Clown' with the white face. He also introduced the modern clown to the world and was unusually skilful at lampooning figures of the day. To this day, on every first Sunday in February a memorial service is held for Grimaldi at the Holy Trinity church, Dalston. (*Oxford National Dictionary of Biography*)

1939: Sung, one of the three pandas acquired by London Zoo in 1938, died aged about three. (Zoological Society)

DECEMBER 19TH

1666: George Villiers, Duke of Buckingham, had a serious tussle with the Marquess of Dorchester in the House of Lords during a conference between the two houses. Buckingham pulled off the Marquess' periwig and Dorchester also 'had much of the duke's hair in his hand'. Clarendon opined that no misdemeanours so flagrant had ever before offended the deputy of the House of Lords. Both offenders were sent to cool down in the Tower, but were released after apologising. (*Victoria County Histories*)

1783: William Pitt became the youngest Prime Minister on this day at the age of twenty-four years and 205 days.

1863: The first ever game of football was played at Mortlake, between Barnes and Richmond – it was a draw. (Football Association)

1932: The BBC's first Empire Service broadcast was made on shortwave radio. It would later change its name to BBC World Service. (BBC)

1974: Five people were injured by an IRA bomb at Selfridges. (*Daily Mail*)

DECEMBER 20TH

1688: A very violent frost began which lasted until 6 February. Its extremity was so great that the pools were frozen at least 18in thick. The Thames was so frozen that a great street from Temple to Southwark was built with shops and all manner of things were sold. There was also bull-baiting and a great many shows and tricks to be seen. (Samuel Pepys)

1860: Dan Leno, a theatre actor and Music Hall comedian, was born in St Pancras into a stage family. He became best known as a pantomime dame, most notably as Dame Durden in *Jack and the Beanstalk*.

2010: Abnormally low temperatures froze planes in their parking stands at Heathrow on Saturday 18 December, but on this day snow virtually shut the airport. All arrivals were cancelled and only seven flights were allowed out, which saw passengers sleeping on terminal floors, while others sought hotel rooms. (*Daily Mail*)

DECEMBER 21ST

1497: Shene Palace, where the Royal Family were settled for Christmas, was destroyed by fire on this evening. (City of London Records Office)

1552: 'Rode to Tyburn to be hanged for Robbery done on Hownslow Heath three tall men and a lacquey.' (Henry Machyn)

1791: Richmond House in Whitehall, fronting the river, used by the Duke of Richmond to exhibit his collection of antiques, was destroyed by fire. (*Morning Post*)

1842: Pentonville Prison in Islington was opened. It was called the 'Model Prison' and the aim was to contain men in jail, although many would be transported to Australia where conditions were far from model. (*Victoria County Histories*)

1846: Robert Liston, the 'Fastest Knife in the West End', who could amputate a leg in two and a half minutes, carried out the first operation in the United Kingdom using ether, amputating the leg above the knee of Fred Churchill. His comment was, 'This Yankee dodge sure beats mesmerism'. (*The Times*)

DECEMBER 22ND

1907: Edith Margaret Emily Ashcroft was born in Croydon on this day and by the age of sixteen had decided to become an actress. Peggy Ashcroft would become a professional actress in 1926 and one of the great stage actresses of the twentieth century. She was also a great artist in front of the cameras, most notably in *Caught on a Train* by Stephen Poliakoff. (*Oxford Dictionary of National Biography*)

1974: The London home of former Prime Minister Edward Heath at Victoria was bombed. A 2lb bomb was thrown on to the first-floor balcony by a man who then escaped in a Ford Cortina. The front door and windows were damaged. Luckily Mr Heath was not at home. (*Daily Telegraph*)

2003: The London Frost Fair was revived with a one-day festival alongside the river at Bankside – known as the Bankside Winter Festival. It has since grown and is modelled on Christmas markets featuring stalls and Christmas events. The 2008 festival lasted a whole week. (*Evening Standard*)

DECEMBER 23RD

1834: On this day Joseph Hansom, an architect (1803-82), registered the design of a 'Patent Safety Cab'. Larger wheels and a lower axle led to fewer accidents. He sold the patent for £10,000 but was never paid! The 'Hansom' cab was sold worldwide. (Patent Office)

———◆———

1919: The Sex Disqualification (Removal) Act 1919 became law on this day when it received Royal Assent. The Act enabled women to enter the legal profession, the civil service and to become jurors. Senior positions, however, remained closed to them and they could be excluded from juries if cases were deemed too sensitive.

———◆———

1970: The murder mystery play *The Mousetrap* by Agatha Christie began as *Three Blind Mice*, a radio play, in 1947. It began its West End run in 1952 and on this day had its 7,511th consecutive performance, breaking the world record for the longest running play. (*Daily Telegraph*)

———◆———

2011: Hammersmith Flyover was closed due to 'chloride contamination' which affected businesses London-wide and travel to Heathrow Airport. (*The Times*)

DECEMBER 24TH

1582: London Bridge Waterworks began piping 'fresh' water to private houses. (City of London Records Office)

———◆◆———

1832: The thirteen-year-old Princess Victoria at Buckingham Palace recorded in her diary, 'After dinner … We then went into the drawing room … There were two large round tables on which were placed two trees hung with lights and sugar ornaments'.

———◆◆———

1904: The New London Coliseum in St Martin's Lane opened, designed by Frank Mitcham. It boasted the first revolving stage in the UK. (*Daily Mail*)

———◆◆———

1933: The 'Codex Sinaiticus', one of the oldest Greek manuscripts in the Bible, purchased from the USSR by the British Museum for £100,000, arrived in London. (*The Times*)

———◆◆———

1997: A *Mirror* journalist bought about 2 grams of cannabis from the seventeen-year-old son of the Home Secretary, Jack Straw. On this day the police confirmed that the boy had been arrested on suspicion of supplying it.

DECEMBER 25TH

1066: William 'the Bastard' Duke of Normandy was crowned William I in Westminster Abbey.

————•◆•————

1781: Thomas Hardy, a shoemaker, had his shop and house 'stripped of boots, shoes and his and his wife's clothes'. (City of London Records Office)

————•◆•————

1864: This day marks the inauguration of the traditional Christmas swim in the Serpentine Lake in Hyde Park. (*The Times*)

————•◆•————

1950: A group of four Scottish students took the Stone of Scone from Westminster Abbey to return it to Scotland. The stone broke into two pieces in transit, but was professionally repaired once it had been recovered. (*Daily Mail*)

————•◆•————

1952: The Ambassadors Theatre premiered a detective story turned into a play, *The Mousetrap* by Agatha Christie – it is still running! (*Daily Mail*)

Queen Elizabeth II made her first Christmas broadcast. Her first televised broadcast was in 1957. (BBC)

DECEMBER 26TH

1871: *Thespis* premiered in London at the Gaiety Theatre. It was a success and closed on 8 March 1872. Advertised as 'an entirely original Grotesque Opera in two acts', no musical score was ever published and most of the music has been lost. (*The Times*)

———◆———

1886: Olympia opened its doors – John Whiteley, its creator, envisaged building the country's longest covered show centre. He commissioned Henry Cole to design it. Today ten cast-iron columns support a 115ft high roof at its apex, with a 1,200-ton frame, 25 tons of glass and 75 tons of zinc. A suite tacked onto the north was named the Prince's Apartments, and was reputedly for Prince Edward's dalliances. (*Victoria County Histories*)

———◆———

1913: A large hippodrome designed by Bertie Crewe was opened at Golders Green. It began as a Variety Hall, but by 1923 was used as a try-out theatre for productions intended for the West End. (*Daily Mail*)

———◆———

1976: The Sex Pistols recorded 'God Save The Queen' at Wessex Studios, a converted Victorian church hall in Highbury New Park.

DECEMBER 27TH

1750: A large Norway bear was baited by two large dogs in a booth in Tottenham Road. (*Gentleman's Magazine*)

1813: Thick smog, smelling of coal tar, blanketed London for eight days. Some said it spread as far as the North Downs, south of London. It was thickest in the East End where the density of factories and homes was greater than almost anywhere else. People claimed you could not see from one side of the street to the other. (*Morning Post*)

1904: *Peter Pan*, J.M. Barrie's play, debuted at the Duke of York's Theatre with Nina Boucicault, the daughter of playwright Dion Boucicault, in the title role. It had originally appeared in a section of *The Little White Bird*, a novel written by Barrie for adults in 1902. (*The Times*)

1963: *The Times* music critics named John Lennon and Paul McCartney as the outstanding composers of 1963. Richard Buckle would later proclaim them as the 'greatest composers since Beethoven'.

DECEMBER 28TH

1065: Westminster Abbey was inaugurated. Pope Nicholas II constituted it the place for the inauguration of the Kings of England.

————◆————

1594: The first performance of Shakespeare's *A Comedy of Errors* took place in the hall of Gray's Inn on this day.

————◆————

1802: On this Tuesday morning a young man discovered the corpse of the Dulwich Hermit, Samuel Matthews, outside the entrance to his cave in Dulwich Woods. His murderer was never discovered.

————◆————

1918: Constance Markievicz, *née* Gore-Booth, was an Irish Sinn Féin, Fianna Fail politician, and a suffragette and socialist who was imprisoned in Holloway. On this day she became the first woman to be elected in a General Election, as Member of Parliament for the constituency of Dublin St Patrick's. However, in line with Sinn Féin's abstentionist policy, she would not stay in the House of Commons. This election was hugely important, because it was the first where nearly all adult men and some women could vote. (*Oxford Dictionary of National Biography*)

DECEMBER 29TH

1860: HMS *Warrior*, the first armour-plated, iron-hulled warship, built for the Royal Navy, was launched on this day. The ship froze on the shipway and six tugs were needed to haul her into the Thames. Although completed in 1861, HMS *Warrior*, the biggest warship along with the *Black Prince*, and the most powerful in the world, never saw active service. (*Illustrated London News*)

———◆———

1940: Dubbed the 'Second Great Fire of London', on this day George Greenwell of the *Daily Mirror* saw St Bride's, Fleet Street, in flames; incendiaries were bouncing off the windows, ledges and rooftops of St Paul's. For twelve hours of the night, the Luftwaffe dropped more than 24,000 high-explosive bombs. This was the largest area of continuous Blitz destruction anywhere in Britain. The raid was timed to coincide with a very low tide, making it difficult for fire-fighters to get water.

———◆———

1966: Pink Floyd appeared at the Marquee in Wardour Street. (*Evening Standard*)

DECEMBER 30TH

1866: 'An unlucky fire at the Crystal Palace reduced the tropical department and consumed a whole zoo of birds and animals, comprising monkeys, chimpanzees, parrots, hummingbirds and a hippopotamus. Had it not been for the screen between this section and the rest of the mighty building, created for the purpose of keeping that especially heated region apart … the masterpiece would have been wrecked. Henceforth the Crystal Palace was a lop-sided structure, its beautiful symmetry destroyed.' (*London and Londoners in the 1850s and 1860s,* Alfred Rosling Bennett, 1924)

———•—•———

1906: The son of actor-producer Sir Herbert Beerbohm-Tree and his mistress Carol Pinney Reed, Carol Reed was born in Putney and showed an early interest in acting. His notable directorial successes were *The Third Man* and *Oliver!* (*Oxford Dictionary of National Biography*)

———•—•———

1981: The Fribourg & Treyer snuff shop on the Haymarket, long the destination of snuff-takers, pipe-smokers and seekers of luxury cigarettes, closed its doors for the last time. Its name and stock were purchased by Imperial Tobacco. (*Daily Telegraph*)

31st December

1661: Samuel Pepys penned his New Year's resolution: 'I have newly taken a solemn oath about abstaining from plays and wine, which I am resolved to keep according to the letter of the oath I keep by me'.

———•◆•———

1853: A life-sized concrete model of an iguanodon, one of several models of extinct dinosaurs made by Benjamin Waterhouse Hawkins of the Crystal Palace Co., was placed at Sydenham Park. It was so large that a twenty-strong dinner party was held inside. (*The Times*)

———•◆•———

1923: The last service for the deaf and dumb at St Saviour's church at No. 419 Oxford Street, W1, was held on this day. Opened in 1874, the Grosvenor Estate was anxious to regain the site for redevelopment at the end of the Church's lease – which is precisely what it did! (*The Times*)

———•◆•———

1999: The British Airways London Eye was formally opened by the Prime Minister Tony Blair. It was only opened to the public, because of technical problems, on 9 March 2000. (*The Times*)